Multi-Faith
Britain

This book is dedicated to the memory of my father George Hart who was always supportive of my writing and who died last year. I would like to thank Ken Moody for his careful assistance in editing and John Hunt and all at O Books for their encouragement and hard work.

Multi-Faith
Britain

An experiment in worship

David A Hart
Preface by the Bishop of Derby

BOOKS

Copyright © 2002 O Books
Text © 2002 David A Hart
Cover: Andrew Milne Design
Typography: Jim Weaver

ISBN 1 903816 08 4

Write to:
John Hunt Publishing Ltd
46A West Street
Alresford
Hampshire SO24 9AU
UK

The rights of the contributors to this work have been asserted in accordance with the Copyright, Designs and Patents Act 1988.

A CIP catalogue record for this book is available from the British Library.

Printed in Guernsey, Channel Islands

Visit us on the Web at: www.o-books.net

List of contributors

Dan Cohn-Sherbok is a rabbi and Professor of Religions at the University of Wales.

Don Cupitt is Fellow of Emmanuel College Cambridge.

Ataullah Siddiqui is Senior Research Fellow at the Islamic Foundation, Markfield, and co-edits the journal *Encounters: Journal of Inter-Cultural Perspectives.*

David A Hart is an Anglican priest and Senior Lecturer in Religious Studies at the University of Derby. He is Development Co-ordinator for Religious and Pastoral Services, and Secretary to the World Congress of Faiths. He divides his time between Britain and India.

Balbinder Singh Bhogal is Lecturer in Buddhism and Sikhism at Derby University.

Pamela Sutton teaches at Derby High School. She chairs the Religious and Pastoral Services Committee at the University of Derby.

Steven Rumelhart is a graduate of Derby University and member of the Druid Order.

Manos Hatzimovos is a graduate of Derby University and works as a Vodaphone style manager in London.

Philip Knight teaches Religious Studies at Geoffrey Chaucer School and Kent College Canterbury.

Benjamin E. Kerr-shaw studied at Ecclesbourne School, Derby, and begins Theology and Religious Studies at Clare College Cambridge later this year.

Philip Henry is Buddhist Adviser to the University of Derby and is researching engaged Buddhism.

Arani Sen is an Anglican priest working in Stepney.

Paul Weller is Professor of Inter-Religious Relations at Derby University. He edits *Religions in the UK: a Multifaith Directory.*

Contents

Acting it Out

Preface

By the Rt Revd Jonathan Bailey,
Bishop of Derby

Multi-Faith Britain is a description of the current situation in 2002. There can be no turning back from a pluralist society involving many faiths and cultures, within which our faiths have to negotiate their own relationships, and their own place within the state. Within Britain, there is of course a variety of experiences of what this means. Whereas the areas around the Metropolis and the Midlands are very mixed, there are still areas, especially at the geographical edges of the country, where the time of a more homogenous culture hangs on. But not perhaps for long, and at any rate we should all prepare ourselves to move around in an increasingly mobile employment market. Increasingly, Britain is part of a global village of many tribes. Derby is more or less central within England, with a population which has benefited largely from Indian migration over the past half a century. We have had the mayor, chief citizen, of Derby elected from Sikh, Muslim and Hindu communities – which tells a story of inclusiveness and opportunity. Naturally, we have not been without our problems. As part of the repercussions of what happened in North-East India in 1992, an incident within the Hindu temple here led religious leaders to meet together and to plan ways in which they could be seen to be co-operating across their traditional divides.

The University was being founded at that time by an amalgamation of previously local colleges and educational institutes of further and higher learning. As a new university, Derby neither had the resources nor the inclination to construct a 'church row' of synagogue/temple/mosque/gurdwara among its new buildings. So through a challenge issued by local religious leaders meeting with University members, its Directorate invited them in 1995 to explore the possibility of organising a campaign to build a 'village of spaces' on the main university campus, as a separate enterprise planned, organised and run by the seven covenanting religions. Those were then Bahai, Buddhist, Christian, Jewish, Hindu, Muslim and Sikh. Planning permission was sought and granted from the local city council, which was also prepared to become 'stakeholder' in the project. A professional fundraiser was appointed to help raise the target of £3 million to build and endow the Centre, and a Development Co-ordinator was appointed by the University. I was asked to chair the Board of Trustees who will oversee the governance of the project. We were offered in 2001 funding of £1.3 million from the Millennium Commission. We still need £250,000 to enable the builders to construct. I would like to ask readers to consider helping us fulfil our dream. 'The Multi-Faith Centre at Derby University' names the registered charity to which cheques can be made out and sent to Eileen Fry, The Project Manager, The University of Derby, Kedleston Road, Derby DE22 1GB. Programmes of events are already up and running and details can be sought from e.fry@derby.ac.uk.

This book is a collection of chapters with different views and understandings around the prospect of a multi-faith Britain. They come from the parallel worlds of religious scholarship and practice. The contributors are not all from Derby, though all of the writers are cognisant and supportive of the project. None of the sentiments expressed has any 'official' status within the construction of our Centre – a lot of the fine detail of that remains to be negotiated. Our principles are, however, clear: we shall provide an open forum where respect for the other and listening to others' stories will be part of our core business. We have already published *Religions in the UK: a multi-faith directory*. We will publish more. We will eat and drink together and celebrate our friendships. We hope to provide something of what Prince Charles has characterised as a 'flagship' for inter-faith activities. As he has said, such activities are necessarily part of a civilised society in the 21st century.

Introduction

This is a book for our times and our place. It is written for and by citizens of the United Kingdom to our fellow citizens who are living in a country that now consists of peoples who trace their routes all over the world. It has not been an easy journey but there is little doubt that we have arrived. Despite the occasional outburst from a Conservative politician, the political establishment is now in favour of a multi-racial society and certainly in its stated positions wishes to affirm the work and contributions of Asians, Africans and others who have made their home within British society.

Tandoori curries have overtaken fish and chips as 'the' British cuisine according to Foreign Secretary Robin Cook. The skyline of the major cities in Britain – London, Glasgow, Cardiff, Leicester, Bradford, Birmingham – now has a new horizon shaped not only by the familiar spires and towers of churches but also by the domes and minarets of mosques. Hindu and Sikh temples of lavish proportion built in the last few years in London have become focuses of Indian cultural and religious pilgrimage in a way never glimpsed beforehand on these shores. Very wealthy and successful Asians run major businesses in the catering, fashion, building, and mobile-phone trades. One of the leading peers in the House of Lords is a young Asian businessman only in his 40s, another Lord Spiritual born and educated in Pakistan is a leading candidate for the top position in the Church of England. In cities and boroughs throughout the 1990s, newly formed Councils of Faiths have come together, very often under the chairing auspices of the Mayoralty, and have paralleled traditional Councils of Churches, formed in the ecumenical movement of the 1960s. They support and sponsor civic events and remembrances, such as war memorials and Holocaust Days. Religious Studies curricula have altered beyond recognition within a generation, from the remembrance of the 16 chapters of the Gospel of Saint Mark, to an examination of the practices and dogmas of seven main world faiths and an introduction to the wonders of ethical and philosophical thought. And these courses and their examinations have become more popular than ever before in both state and private schools. In the world of literature, a sea change happened in the 1980s when writing in English from India was made more widely available in Britain, and authors of Muslim, Sikh and Hindu origins became familiar household names.

Naturally, it takes some adjustment for all of us to realise that our own faith is no longer the unquestioned centre of the universe. Within Christian theology, this 'Copernican shift' has been reflected in the life and teaching of Professor John Hick, above all in his book *An Interpretation of Religion* (1989). He has argued that we have to shift our perspective from an exclusive understanding of our faith and its truth-claims, through a more inclusive understanding of its dogmas, to a final pluralist reading that sees the relation of the faiths analogously to the positioning of the planets around the sun. There is a central 'transcendence', which can also be defined as 'the Real'. All faiths are human attempts to perceive that quality. The Real cannot, Hick argues, be defined, certainly not as 'God' as there are ideologies such as Jainism and Communism that share the characteristics of other religions without holding to the existence of a separate divine being. But, Hick says, the continued religious quest of humankind is one that, if it does not speak directly of, nevertheless witnesses to, the existence of that divine reality that lies at the centre of our universe.

With modifications, this position remains essentially that of most of the influential academics writing in the United Kingdom at this time. The late Ninian Smart started from an Anglican theological base and through global study and marriage to a Japanese wife, founded the first multi-faith undergraduate course in Religious Studies in the 1970s at Lancaster University, and took the argument further East than previous Western scholars, engaging especially with Buddhism and Confucianism and Taoism in his overview of world philosophies and religions. Smart also admired the work of the Reverend Sun Myung Moon and his Unification Church in Korea in its attempt since its foundation in 1954 through marriage blessings and interfaith dialogue to bring into a new form of visible unity the religious faiths of the world. From 1997 Moon renamed his church as the Inter-Religious and International Federation for World Peace.

John Hinnells has spent most of his academic life studying religions which lay outside his original base, also of Anglicanism, specialising particularly in the ancient religion of Persia, first enunciated by the prophet Zarathustra born possibly 6,000 years before the common era. Popularly known as Zoroastrianism in Iran and the Parsis in dispersion in India, this is one of the oldest founts of religious imagery based on the four elements – *Khorshed* (sun), *Mehr* (the heavenly light), *Mahabokhta* (the moon), *Avan* (water) and *Adar* (fire). In editing many collections of essay, Hinnells has come to question the category of 'world religion'. He argues for a multi-faith approach to religious studies to which he has contributed in a glowing career, which has spanned religious studies departments in Manchester, the School of Oriental and Asian Studies (London) and currently at Derby University.

On the more popular level, Karen Armstrong has widened her religious perspective from that of a Roman Catholic convert and a concern for 'the Gospel for woman' to a more recent focus on the prophet Mohammed (peace be upon him) and the Buddha, the latter book dedicated to her sister who converted to that particular path. Armstrong argues for a liberal and wider understanding of religions from the perspective of what she calls a 'second Axial age' in which the world-perspective is undergoing fast and seismic changes, which will inevitably have far-reaching outcomes in the reformulation of all credal statements, and which will be opposed in a contrary realignment of religious perspectives by those who like to reassert the fundamentals of their particular perspective, and read those to be in basic opposition to the presuppositions of the dominant ideology they take to be a liberal secularism.

In my earlier book *One Faith? Non-realism and the World of Faiths* (1995) I presented an understanding of five world religions which saw them not as competing theological positions but as contiguous collections of human stories of the deities in conversation with humanity. Using the perspective in contemporary philosophy of religion that has been developed in the writings of Don Cupitt, I presented the possibilities of 'passing over' from one religious faith to another and enriching one's spiritual perspective from such a 'transgression'. In an appendix, I gave an actual example of a multi-faith form of worship, which had been used to rededicate the work of Leicestershire County Council. The new chairman, who came from a Quaker background, wished to be inclusive of insights from world traditions in an act of worship which had the County and its representatives welcome him into his year of office.

In this symposium, I wish to carry through some of the implications on the two levels within which we all live and move and have our being – namely, thinking it through (in the world of ideas and 'justifications') and also acting it out (in the public world and in our ethical practice). So in the first section, I have invited scholars from seven world faiths to look at their own faith-perspective, and assess how far, in its founders' vision, in its scriptures, in its teachings and in its practice, it is open to the more liberal approach to religions that is now possible in a multi-faith society such as the United Kingdom in the 21st century. I hope it is self-evident that these scholars, though with academic credentials, are not 'authorities' in their faiths and they argue from their particular perspective which clearly differs on the theological spectrum from person to person.

In the second section, I have asked individuals who are engaged in current multi-faith practice in the United Kingdom to share their experiences and insights with others. I have deliberately chosen these from the right side of 40, with two of them specifically members of our Youth Forum at The Multi-Faith Centre. Their practices are testing the boundaries previously drawn. But I hope that they can provide bold examples for others to follow in their own spheres. There is everything to be gained or lost in this experiment in worship, which we celebrate in this volume and to which feast I would like to invite you, the reader, if you have not as yet taken your rightful place. Many more have joined than we often imagine, if only because of the incidence of inter-faith marriages within which two individuals and their respective families often find themselves entering inter-faith dialogue. These happened through personal encounter and a process of growth of understanding and love for each other. This today should not be just tolerated, but embraced as a unique opportunity for much sharing and mutual learning for all.

Religion, of course, is famously described as either the best poison or the best medicine, depending upon how it is administered. Recently the vision of a harmonious multi-faith Britain has been severely tested, not only in rioting in Burnley and in Oldham but also here in Derby. Letters were circulated which attempted to stir up enmity between young people of Sikh and Muslim communities respectively, by suggesting how inter-faith relationships could be used to convert individuals by stealth and force to another religion. Such irreligious suggestions were roundly condemned by religious and community leaders, but not before significant personal damage had been wreaked by individuals inspired by the politics of hatred. Questions were asked in the House of Commons, and the Home Secretary appealed to the communities in Derby to reach an understanding with one another over this issue. 2001 has also seen the testing of multi-faith tolerance on the international level with one date, 11th September, becoming a cipher for an attack on all dialogue and attempts to proceed by discussion rather than force.

It has been no easier this year. The situation in the Middle East seems to go from bad to worse. We continually wonder about the peace in Northern Ireland and hope for the best. In India, ten years later, the Ayodhya affair seems to rumble on in Hindu-Muslim confrontation, and as I write this, I read of the situation in Gujarat as reported on the front page of my newspaper: 'On the highways, gangs of young men armed with sticks and iron rods stopped all cars to ask whether Muslims or Hindus were inside. Only Hindus were allowed to proceed.' In a global village such news relayed directly to our TV screens in the United Kingdom will do nothing to further community relations here. Nevertheless, we do have to realise and to emphasise that our country and its traditions of tolerance should provide a more inclusive environment. For this reason a 'copycat' approach by the communities here is really inappropriate to our situation and the opportunities for common cause which are now available to all communities here in Britain.

Valuable is the Parekh Report *The Future of Multi-Ethnic Britain* published by the Runnymeade Trust in 2000. Introducing its findings to a conference at Leicester, the first city in the United Kingdom which is on course to have an ethnic majority population by 2005, Robin Richardson cited the words of poet Ben Okri, that 'stories are the secret reservoir of values: change the stories individuals and nations live by and tell themselves and you change the individuals and nations. If they tell themselves stories that are lies, they will suffer the future consequences of those lies. If they tell themselves stories that face their own truths, they will free their futures for future flowerings.' Parekh argues for a move away from the discourse of majority/minority and homogeneity to one of a community of communities and citizens. All communities are changing and complex; changing in response to internal dynamics, interactions with others and globalisation. The boundaries between communities are fuzzy and people live with what Peggy Morgan has called 'multiple competencies'. Britain ... meaning Derby, Leicester, Bradford and so on ... are the names of the spaces where many communities meet, negotiate, mingle and learn about both their common agenda and what makes a good society. By thinking it all through and acting it out, we may be able to achieve a new way of networking which will also be a new way of being peoples of faith.

Lord God of Many Glorious Names

Words by David Mowbray, Vicar of Darley Abbey
(Written for The Multi-Faith Centre at the University of Derby)
Tune: Brother James' Air

1. Within this sacred, special place
    We gather now to pray;
    Lord God of many glorious names
    Bless us with peace today.
    >   Lord God of many glorious names
    >   bless us with peace today.

2. Within these walls, a vessel for
    Faith's treasures that we bring,
    Lord God of every race on earth
    Yours is the praise we sing.
    >   Lord God of every race on earth
    >   Yours is the praise we sing.

3. Within this space may all engage
    With heart as well as mind;
    Creator and Sustainer God,
    Help us explore and find.
    >   Creator and Sustainer God,
    >   help us explore and find.

4. Within our city, let respect
   for all traditions grow;
   God of compassion and of love,
   Such gifts on us bestow.
   > God of compassion and of love
   > such gifts on us bestow.

5. Within our world, our universe,
   Wherever feet have trod
   May we be moved to do something
   That's beautiful for God.
   > May we be moved to do something
   > that's beautiful for God.

© David Mowbray *Jubilate Hymns*

Judaism and the Universe of Faiths

Dan Cohn-Sherbok

In contemporary society with its multiplicity of faiths, there has been an increasing interest in the relationship between the world's religions. Within the Jewish community there currently exists a flourishing dialogue between Jewish and Christian thinkers as well as an embryonic development of Jewish-Muslim dialogue. Nonetheless, with few exceptions, Jewish writers have not seriously considered the place of Judaism in the context of humanity's religious experience. This is regrettable since there are urgent reasons why Jewish theologians need to explore the relationship between Judaism and the universe of faiths. Thus, this chapter seeks to develop a new approach to Jewish interfaith dialogue, drawing on resources within the Jewish tradition.

Judaism and Other Faiths

Through the centuries Judaism has adopted a relatively tolerant attitude toward other religions. In the biblical period the ancient Israelites were encouraged to view the gods of other peoples as non-entities; in this respect ancient Israelite faith was exclusivist in orientation. Yet foreign peoples were not condemned for their pagan practices. Although the religion of the Jewish people was perceived as the one true faith, there was no harsh condemnation of idolatry. Furthermore, it was the conviction of the prophets that in the end of days all nations would recognise that the God of the Israelites was the Lord of the Universe. There was no compulsion to undertake missions since there was hope even for pagan peoples in the unfolding of God's plan of salvation.

In the rabbinic period this tradition of tolerance continued to animate Jewish life. According to the rabbis, all non-Jews who follow the Noachide Laws are viewed as acceptable to God. In this context even those who engage in polytheistic practices are admissible as long as the gods they worship are conceived as symbolically pointing to the one God. In these rabbinic sources is the beginning of a form of inclusivism in which foreign peoples, despite their seeming polytheism, are seen as 'anonymous monotheists'.

In the medieval period writers such as Rabbenu Tam applied this rabbinic conception of symbolic intermediacy to Christian believers. In his opinion Christianity is not idolatry since Christians are monotheists despite their belief in the Trinity. Other writers including Judah Halevi formulated an even more tolerant form of Jewish inclusivism. For these thinkers Christians as well as Muslims play an important role in God's plan for humanity by spreading the message of monotheism.

This positive stance toward other faiths continued into the early modern period as a result of the impact of the Enlightenment. In the 18th century the Jewish philosopher Moses Mendelssohn argued that the Jewish people were the recipients of a divine revelation consisting of ritual and moral law. Nevertheless, Mendelssohn was convinced that God's reality could be discerned through human reason. Thus all human beings are capable of discerning God's nature and activity. During this period other thinkers offered a sympathetic appreciation of Christianity while at the same time adhering to the belief that Judaism is the superior religion. The French scholar Joseph Salvador, for example, believed that in the future Christians would help to bring about a new philosophical religion resembling Judaism; in this respect his positive evaluation of Christianity provided a form of Jewish inclusivism tempered by the scientific spirit of the age. Similarly, the German reform rabbi Abraham Geiger argued that Christianity embraces God's revelation to his chosen people, yet Judaism constitutes the ideal faith for the modern age.

From the late 18th century, during the age of Emancipation, Jewish thinkers grappled with the currents of Western thought and in their different ways offered a positive evaluation of Christianity and Islam. Pre-eminent among 19th-century Jewish writers, the German theologian Samuel Hirsch maintained that throughout history Judaism had struggled to overcome the threat of paganism. According to Hirsch, Christianity has an important role in this struggle but the Jewish faith, as the purest form of monotheism, is humanity's ultimate hope for the future.

A similar form of Jewish inclusivism was espoused by the German reform rabbi Solomon Formstecher who argued that even though Judaism is the ultimate form of the religious life, Christianity and Islam play an important part in the unfolding of God's plan. Such a view was also advanced by another German thinker of this age, Solomon Ludwig Steinheim, who viewed Christianity as furthering God's eschatological scheme. An even more positive assessment of Christianity was fostered by the British Jewish writer Claude Montefiore who stressed that God reveals himself in different ways throughout history. For Montefiore the Christian faith is one such disclosure, and Jews can be enlightened by a knowledge of the New Testament.

More recently a number of Jewish scholars have advanced a sympathetic approach to the world's faiths. The Jewish theologian Louis Jacobs, for example, in his *A Jewish Theology* stresses that Judaism has always endorsed the view that there is only one God and that the Torah has not been superseded by any other religious tradition. Such a conviction, he believes, compels the Jews to declare that the positions of other faiths are false if they contradict the Jewish faith. Yet despite such an uncompromising stance, he contends that it would be a mistake for Jews to conclude that God has not revealed himself to others or that other religions do not contain any truth. On the contrary, the position one should adopt is that there is more truth in Judaism than in other religions.

Another contribution to this topic is by the Israeli Orthodox theologian David Hartman. In *On the Possibilities of Religious*

Pluralism from a Jewish Point of View, he maintains that the Bible contains two covenants: that of Creation and that of Sinai. The Creation covenant is with all humanity; it is universal and for all generations. The Sinai covenant on the other hand is with Israel; it is a parallel covenant and embraces other communities. On the basis of this scheme, Hartman argues that God has revealed himself to different groups of peoples at various times in history.

Another Orthodox thinker, Norman Solomon, discusses the issue of religious pluralism in *Judaism and World Religion*. Here he argues that Judaism is a religion with a mission to all people. In times of persecution, he states, this universal goal has been overlooked; yet it has never disappeared. In bad times it focuses on the messianic task; in enlightened eras it is expressed in the Jewish quest to work for the improvement of humanity. In pursuing this goal, the 'covenant of Noah' (as expressed in the Noachide laws), offers a pattern to seek for others without requiring their conversion to Judaism. What is demanded instead is faithfulness to the highest principles of justice and morality. In this context, the dialogue of faiths becomes an imperative which emerges through our common mission with other world religions.

Given the largely tolerant attitude of Judaism to other faiths from ancient times to the present, arguably Jews should not move beyond the forms of inclusivism advanced by these contemporary thinkers. However, to use the model of the universe of faiths formulated by the Protestant theologian John Hick, a Copernican Revolution is now required in our understanding of religion. In the past even the most liberal Jewish thinkers retained the conviction that Judaism contains the fullest divine disclosure; while recognising the inherent value of other religions, particularly Christianity, they were convinced that Judaism is humanity's future hope. In the modern world, however, where Jews continually come into contact with adherents of other religious traditions, it is difficult to sustain such a narrow vision and a revolution is currently required in our understanding of the universe of faiths. Instead of placing Judaism at the centre of the world's religions, a theocentric model should be adopted. Such a transformation demands a paradigm shift from a Judeo-centric to a theo-centric conception of religious history. On this basis, the world's religions should be understood as different human responses to the one divine reality.

A Jewish Theology of World Religions

Throughout the history of the Jewish faith there has been a conscious awareness of a distinction between God-as-he-is-in-himself and human conceptions of the Divine. Scripture, for example, frequently cautions against describing God anthropomorphically. Thus Deuteronomy states: 'Therefore take good heed to yourselves. Since you saw no form on the day that the Lord spoke to you at Horeb out of the midst of the fire' (Deut 4:15). Again, Exodus 33:20,21 declares: 'And he said, "You cannot see my face; for man shall not see me, and live." And the Lord said, "Behold there is a place by me where you shall stand".'

In rabbinic literature there are comparable passages which suggest that human beings should refrain from attempting to describe God. Thus the Palestinian teacher Abin said: 'When Jacob of the village of Neboria was in Tyre, he interpreted the verse "For thee, silence is praise, O God" to mean that silence is the ultimate praise of God. It can be compared to a jewel without price: however high you appraise it, you will undervalue it.' In another Talmudic passage a story is told of the prayer reader who was rebuked by the scholar Hanina. The reader praised God by listing as many of his attributes as he could. When he finished Hanina asked if he had exhausted the praises of God. Hanina then said that even the three attributes 'The Great', 'The Valiant' and 'The Tremendous' could not legitimately be used to describe God were it not for the fact that Moses used them and they subsequently became part of the Jewish liturgy.

The latter development of such a view was continued by both Jewish philosophers and mystics. In his treatise, *Duties of the Heart*, for example, the 11th-century philosopher Bahya Ibn Pakudah argued that the concept of God's unity involves the negation from God of all human and infinite limitations. According to Bahya, if we wish to ascertain the nature of anything, we must ask *if* it is, and *what* it is. Of God, however, it is possible to ask only *if* he is. Once having established his existence, it is not possible to go on to enquire about his nature, since it is beyond understanding.

In the *Guide for the Perplexed*, the 12th-century Jewish philosopher Moses Maimonides focused on the concept of negative attributes. For Maimonides the ascription to God of positive attributes is a form of idolatry because it suggests that his attributes are co-existent with him. To say that God is one, Maimonides contended, is simply a way of negating all plurality from his being. Even when one asserts that God exists, one is simply affirming that his non-existence is impossible. Positive attributes are only admissible if they are understood as referring to God's *acts*. Attributes which refer to his nature, however, are only permissible if they are applied negatively. Moreover, the attributes which refer to God's actions imply only the acts themselves – they do not refer to the emotions from which these actions are generated when performed by human beings.

Like these Jewish philosophers, Jewish mystics advocated a theory of negation in describing God. For these kabbalists the Divine is revealed through the powers which emanate from him. Yet God as he is in himself is the *Ayn Sof* (Infinite). The *Zohar* (Book of Splendour) asserts that the *Ayn Sof* is incomprehensible. It is only through the *sefirot* (divine emanations) that the Divine is manifest in the world. According to the *Zohar* even the higher realms of the Divine – the stages represented by God's will, wisdom and understanding (*Keter, Hokhmah* and *Binah*) – should be understood negatively. Thus God's will, which is represented by the *sefirah Keter,* is referred to as *Ayin* (nothingness). It is so elevated beyond human understanding that it can only be represented by negation. Concerning divine wisdom, represented by *Hokhmah*, the *Zohar* declares that one can ask what it is but should expect no answer.

Here, then, is a theological framework, deeply rooted in the Jewish tradition, which can serve as a basis for a new vision of Jewish theology in the modern age. Acknowledging the limitation of human comprehension, such a way of unknowing reveals that there is no means by which to ascertain the true nature of Divine Reality as-it-is-in-itself. In the end, the doctrines of Judaism must be regarded as human images constructed from within particular social and cultural contexts. The implications of this shift from the absolutism of the Jewish past to a new conception of Jewish theology is radical and far-reaching. Judaism, like all other religions, has advanced absolute, universal claims about the nature of the Divine but, given the limits of our finite understanding of Ultimate Reality, there is no way of attaining complete certitude about the veracity of these beliefs. Divine Reality as-it-is-in-itself transcends human comprehension, and hence it must be admitted that Jewish religious convictions are no different in principle from those found in other religious traditions: all are lenses through which the Ultimate is conceptualised.

Such a view of the Divine in relation to the universe of faiths can be represented by the image of alternative paths ascending a single mountain; each route symbolises a particular religion with Divine Reality floating like a cloud above the mountain top. The routes of these faith communities are all different, yet at various points they intersect: these intersections should be understood as those areas where religious conceptions within the differing traditions complement one another. So, as pilgrims of different faiths ascend to the summit, they will encounter parallels with their own traditions but the Divine Reality they all pursue is in the end attainable by these finite quests. As the Infinite, the Divine Reality is unknowable and incomprehensible.

Such a pluralistic model implies that the conceptions of the Divine in the world's religions are ultimately human images. They represent the myriad ways of approaching the one indescribable Divine Reality. Doctrinal differences reflect differences in the historical, social and cultural factors lying behind these images. Not only does this pluralistic framework offer a more comprehensible theoretical basis for understanding differences between religious systems, it also provides a wider forum for interfaith encounter. Instead of assuming, as Jewish inclusivists have in the past, that Judaism embodies God's all-embracing truth of which other religions possess only a share,

Jewish pluralism encourages Jews to engage in fruitful and enriching dialogue with members of other traditions.

This new model further reflects our current understanding of the world in which no truth is viewed as unchanging. Rather, truth-claims by their very nature must be open to other insights. They prove themselves not by triumphing over other belief systems, but by testing their compatibility with other truths. Such a conception of relational-truth affords a new orientation to our understanding of truth in religion. On this view, religious truth is not static but instead undergoes continual interaction and development.

This model of truth-through-relationship allows each religion to be unique. The truth a religion contains is uniquely important for religious adherents, but it is not true in a universal sense. Religious truth is relevant only for those who subscribe to it. Judaism thus should not be conceived as the one, truth faith for all human beings. Rather, Judaism is true only for the Jewish people. Such a pluralist confessional stance is thus both certain and open-ended. It enables Jews to affirm the uniqueness of their faith while urging them to recognise the validity of other traditions. Here, then, is a new framework for positive encounter and religious harmony. If Jews can free themselves from an absolutist standpoint in which claims are viewed as possessing ultimate and universal truth, the way is open for a radically new vision of Jewish dialogue with the world's faiths and for interfaith encounters at the deepest levels. In previous centuries Jewish theologians asserted that Judaism is the superior tradition; even the most liberal thinkers maintained that in the future humanity would acknowledge the truth of Jewish monotheism. The pursuit of religious truth, however, calls for a global dialogical approach. As the Christian theologian Wilfred Cantwell-Smith remarked:

> The time will soon be with us when a theologian who attempts to work out his position unaware that he does so as a member of a world society in which other theologians equally intelligent, equally devout, equally oral, are Hindus, Buddhists, Muslims and unaware that his readers are likely perhaps to be Buddhists or to have Muslim husbands or Hindu colleagues – such a theologian is as out of date as is one who attempts to

construct an intellectual position unaware that Aristotle has thought about the world or that existentialists have raised new orientations, or unaware that the earth is a minor planet in a galaxy that is vast only by terrestrial standards. Smith, 1962, 123

The formulation of a Jewish global, inter-religious theology is based on two pre-conditions. *First*, Jewish thinkers must learn about religious traditions other than their own. Global theology undertaken from such a vantage point requires theologians to investigate what the world's faiths have experienced and affirmed about the nature of Divine Reality, the phenomenon of religious experience, the nature of the self, the problem of the human condition, and the value of the world. *Secondly*, Jewish theologians should attempt to enter into the thought-world as well as the religious experiences of those of other faiths. This can only be done by becoming a participant in their way of life.

Jewish thinkers must thus enter into the subjectivity of other traditions and bring the resulting insights to bear on their own understanding of religion. Such reflection demands a multi-dimensional, cross-cultural, inter-religious consciousness. Given this quest for a global perspective, those who embrace such openness must insist that the theological endeavour takes place in a trans-religious context. This enterprise requires an encounter in which Jews confront others who hold totally different truth-claims. Such individuals can help Jewish thinkers to discover their own pre-suppositions and underlying principles. In this process Jewish partners should be able to acknowledge the limitations of their own tradition, and as a result make a conscious effort to discover common ground with other faiths. Such an interchange is vital to the formulation of a multi-dimensional theological outlook.

An Agenda for Dialogue

Given the possibility of this type of inter-religious exploration, there are a number of central issues which Jews and adherents of other faiths could fruitfully explore together.

1. *Symbols.* Jews and members of other traditions could profitably

explore the nature of religious symbols as long as neither the Jewish nor the non-Jewish partner maintains that the symbols in their respective faith are superior. Not very much is known about the logic of symbols: we do not understand why people use certain symbols; why they give up others; why they remain unmoved by symbols that members of other faiths find meaningful; why they are moved by a symbol that others find meaningless; and why they are moved by a symbol that others find objectionable. If discussion were to occur across religious lines, it might be possible to attain greater insight into what is involved in religious symbolism.

2. *Worship.* In most religions, worship is a response to the Divine, an acknowledgement of a reality independent of the worshipper. Assuming that neither the Jewish nor the non-Jewish participant in interfaith dialogue maintains that his or her conception of Ultimate Reality is uniquely true, it would be helpful to discuss the ways in which various forms of worship provide some glimpse into the nature of Divine Reality. Furthermore, it might be possible to investigate the ways in which the liturgical features of one tradition could be incorporated into the other. The Passover *Seder*, for example, is viewed by most scholars as the ceremony celebrated at the Last Supper. In this regard it is as much a part of the Christian as the Jewish tradition and could become an element of the Christian liturgy. This is simply one example of the ways in which adherents of different faiths could enrich the liturgical dimensions of each other's traditions.

3. *Ritual.* Like worship, ritual plays a major role in the world's religions, and there are areas worthy of joint investigation as long as neither party adopts an attitude of religious superiority. First, an examination of both formal and elaborate practices and simple actions could reveal the ways in which the believers see their actions as making contact or participating in the Divine. Secondly, a comparative study of ritualistic practice could clarify the ways in which an outer activity mirrors an inner process – a relationship fundamental to the concept of ritualistic behaviour. Thirdly, it might be beneficial to examine the contemplative and mystical activities in different traditions, such as the *Kabbalah* in Judaism, which are understood as disclosing various

aspects of the Divine and enable the practitioner to reach an altered state of consciousness.

4. *Ethics.* Traditional Jews believe that God chose the Jewish nation to be his special people and gave them his law on Mount Sinai. The moral law is thus embodied in immutable, divine commandments. In other faiths, however, ethical values are perceived in a different light. For the traditional Christian, for example, Christ is understood as the end of the Law, thereby superseding the Torah as the mediator between God and human beings. Allowing that both Jews and Christians adopt a more open-minded stance to moral attitudes within their respective traditions, it would be worthwhile to examine Jesus' critique of Pharisaic Judaism. Such an investigation could help to disclose the tension between specific rules and general principles as well as the relationship between action and intention. As far as other faiths are concerned, the exploration of the foundations of alternative ethical systems could result in a deepening of ethical perception.

5. *Society.* Religions are not only systems of belief and practice; they are also organisations which have a communal and social dimension. Given that neither the Jewish nor non-Jewish partner in dialogue assumes that their faith possesses a better organisational structure and a more positive attitude toward modern society, it would be of interest to examine the ways in which each religion understands itself in relation to the world. In addition, since many faiths contain religious hierarchies, an analysis of the nature of institutional structures, the training of leaders and the exercise of authority could clarify the ways in which religious traditions reflect the non-religious characteristics of the societies in which they exist. In the face of modern secularism, such an examination would be of particular consequence since, more than ever before, religions find themselves forced to adapt to a rapidly changing world.

These subject areas by no means exhaust the possibilities for interfaith dialogue, but they do indicate the type of joint activity that could take place.

On the verge of the third millennium Judaism stands on the threshold of a new awakening. Drawing on centuries of tolerance,

Jews will find the way open to formulate a complete reorientation of their faith in relation to other religious traditions. With a shift from inclusivism to pluralism, there is no longer a need to interpret other religions from a Judeo-centric standpoint. Rather, with the Divine at the centre of the universe of faiths, Jewry can acknowledge the inevitable subjectivity of all religious beliefs, including those contained in the Jewish heritage. Jewish pluralism demands the recognition that all religions constitute separate paths to Divine Reality – yet, at the summit of this ascent, the Real as-it-is-in-itself remains beyond human comprehension for it is the cloud of unknowing beyond human grasp. As the *Shekhinah* led the children of Israel for 40 years through the wilderness – always present, always ahead, and always unreachable, so the Divine hovers just beyond the range of human apprehension. If the Jewish people are to remain faithful to the age-old vision of the Word of the Lord going forth from Zion, they must listen to that Word as it comes from many Zions, from Mecca as well as Sinai, from Benares as well as Safed, from Rome as well as Vilna, from Kyoto as well as Jerusalem.

Bibliography

Cantwell-Smith, Wilfred, *The Faith of Other Men*, New York, 1962.

Cohn-Sherbok, Dan, *Judaism and Other Faiths*, Macmillan, 1996.

Hartman, David, *On the Possiblities of Religious Pluralism from a Jewish Point of View*, Immanuel 1983.

Jacobs, Louis, *A Jewish Theology*, New York, 1973.

Knitter, Paul, *No Other Name*, SCM, 1985.

Solomon, Norman, *Judaism and World Religion*, London, 1992.

Christianity and Tolerance

Don Cupitt

Although many people may be surprised to hear it, Christianity was not historically a tolerant faith: indeed, for much of its history it was less tolerant than Islam. According to standard Islamic teaching there have been three 'heavenly religions', Judaism, Christianity and Islam, and although the final revelation of God to the prophet Muhammad has superseded the earlier revelations given through Moses and Jesus, nevertheless classical Islam held that Jews and Christians should be treated with respect and allowed to continue to practise their religions within the House of Faith (that is, Islamic territory). Thus Islam has usually been able to envisage a society in which several distinct religions co-exist peacefully; whereas Christianity in its long medieval period always held itself to be the one and only true religion, and was so interwoven with civil society that any religious dissent was seen as a major threat to society and was liable to be punished by death. As for the Jews, they were probably more at risk of pogroms and persecutions in medieval Latin Christianity than they were during the same period in Islam.

Only after the Protestant Reformation, and the many wars to which it gave rise, did the conditions develop under which people in Europe could begin to see religious toleration as desirable and indeed necessary for the sake of civil peace. In America two of the early colonies, Maryland and Rhode Island, pioneered the idea of a peaceful religiously-plural society in the 1630s and 1640s. In England, the poet John Milton and the philosopher John Locke were advocates of the –

admittedly, rather limited – religious freedom that was finally granted by the Act of Toleration in 1689. After that, the Church of England was still the established state church, of which you had to be a member in order to gain entry to one of the universities or to hold a commission in the Army; but otherwise a wide range of protestant denominations were now tolerated. They included Baptists, Congregationalists, Independents and even Quakers – but not Unitarians or Roman Catholics.

Thus England became one of the first 'multi-faith' countries. In those days different Christian sects were spoken of as different 'religions', which is what Voltaire had in mind when in the 1730s he wrote in praise of English religious toleration, saying humorously that if the English had only two or three religions, they would be at each other's throats; but they have 30, and so they live in peace (*Philosophical Letters*, 1733). If society is divided into a large number of religious sects, one can see that it is not practical for any one of them to dream of being able to wipe out all its rivals. Common sense requires us all to find a basis on which we can co-exist peacefully.

On this pragmatic basis, religious toleration has slowly developed in the West. During the 19th century it was gradually extended in Britain to groups such as Unitarians, the Jews, Roman Catholics and even unbelievers. Gradually, the various prohibitions affecting non-Anglicans have been removed, until today almost the only one left is that a non-Anglican still cannot accede to the Throne – and even that prohibition will probably not remain for much longer.

This history is a necessary background to the new situation that has developed in Britain, especially since the 1950s. A society that has long been multi-faith in the sense of tolerating all kinds and degrees of Christian and Jewish belief and unbelief is now multi-faith in a much wider sense: virtually all of the world's principal religions are now established in Britain, and London has become one of the most ethnically and linguistically diverse cities in the world.

In earlier times the usual way in which great trading cities coped with ethnic and religious diversity was by dividing the city into different quarters, one being assigned to each major group. This pattern can still be seen in the Old City at Jerusalem, and it is not surprising that it is often repeated in modern Western cities, as newly arrived immigrants tend to settle among people of their own background and faith. Cities like London and Liverpool have had 'Chinatowns' and Jewish neighbourhoods for some centuries, and nowadays they have dozens of local clusters of expatriates from almost every part of the world.

These ethnic communities differ very greatly in the energy they put into maintaining and propagating their ancestral faith. The Chinese in diaspora live mainly in small Chinatowns, found in capital cities and major ports everywhere. Most of them are of Cantonese origin, and they maintain some of their domestic religious rituals. But with higher education they tend to become Westernised and drift away, and I do not know of anywhere, apart from San Francisco, where the Chinese in diaspora have built temples like those that are still popular in Hong Kong. But, at the opposite extreme, Muslims in diaspora work hard at maintaining their ancestral language, culture and religion. In Britain, they are now said to have 1,000 mosques and are a very conspicuous presence in society.

Those are the two extremes: the Chinese are low-profile, both politically and religiously, and do not build many temples or set out to propagate their religion, whereas Muslims are in comparison much higher-profile. They are politically active, and have had some success in winning public funding for their own Islamic schools. Furthermore, they are very active in building places of worship, and in presenting their own faith to the wider society as both alive and intellectually challenging. They have made some Western converts, but they do not yet conduct public worship in the English language, and a fully anglicised form of Islamic faith does not yet exist.

This last observation raises the question of how far, even in the three great multicultural 'world' religions of Christianity, Buddhism and Islam, a faith that professes to be universal always remains in practice tied to particular traditions in culture, language and dress. In Britain there has been fully assimilated and anglicised Judaism for many generations, and Roman Catholicism became fully-assimilated during the 20th century. But we are not quite clear about whether there is yet a fully assimilated Western form of Buddhism. There is indeed the long-established Buddhist Society, and there is the (more controversial) Western Buddhist Order, but nobody could say that Buddhism is yet as deeply assimilated into Western culture as it became into Chinese or Japanese culture. Society at large still tends to classify Buddhism with the various 'alternative' or counter-cultural sects and movements that are popular amongst the urban young.

Hinduism is in a somewhat similar position. Since the 19th century there have been many manifestations of middle-class intellectual interest in Hindu thought, in bodies such as the Theosophical Society which so influenced the young Gandhi: but popular Hinduism as actually practised by the people of India is not assimilated at all. In Britain, to outsiders, it seems purely ethnic and no more likely to become assimilated than is the popular Buddhism of (for example) Tibet or Thailand.

In Britain the appeal of Hinduism and Buddhism to outsiders has so far been chiefly intellectual: it has been the appeal of Hindu and Buddhist philosophy and meditation to middle-class intellectual seekers. The cases of Islam and Sikhism are very different. People are on the whole incurious about Muslim and Sikh thought: they like Islamic art and enjoy the popular Islamic culture of the story-tellers, but Islamic literature is otherwise almost unknown; while the entire religion and culture of the Sikhs are almost completely unknown, and few British people have ever even seen a copy of the Adi Granth, the Sikh scriptures. But both the Muslims and the Sikhs have deeply impressed Westerners as religious communities. They have a distinctiveness, a social discipline, a cohesion, a group loyalty and a determination to preserve their own faith that Westerners admire. We may disagree with some of their values, but they are still 'peoples of the Book' in a sense that we too once were, but are no longer.

The distinction that I am drawing here can now be summed up. Westerners who have been drawn to Hinduism especially during the first half of the 20th century, and to Buddhism more recently, have mainly been educated seekers, attracted by the philosophies and the practice of meditation that these faith-traditions offer to the *individual* seeker after salvation. People who are attracted by the Sikhs or by Muslims are rather different: they are drawn to a concrete *community* whose ethos, whose social discipline and whose genuinely deep piety they admire. At its very best, life as an ordinary Muslim in a local community may have a religious simplicity and clarity such as Westerners nowadays expect to find only in a contemplative order of Christian nuns or monks.

The question now arises of how these very disparate faiths are to settle into British society. Britain was historically a Christian country, and remained about 50% practising Christian until the early or mid-19th century. Today the various Christian denominations all survive, but they are much reduced. Some features of the former Christian culture also survive. They are reflected in the civil law (for example) and in the calendar, where AD dating, the observance of Sunday as a day of rest, and the continuing great popularity of Christmas are regular reminders of the Christian past. Most important of all are the great medieval buildings, conspicuous in almost every British community from village to city, which are a painful reminder that our religion once dominated our whole life, whereas today it can scarcely be called more than the leisure pursuit of a small minority of us.

Christians have come down in the world very rapidly, and they find it hard to reconcile themselves to their own diminished status. Nor are they finding it easy to accept that they are now just one group of sects amongst many others in a society that has become *both* predominantly secular *and* highly pluralistic and multi-faith. For much of the time Christians – like many people of other faiths – tend to keep with their own kind, and prefer not to think about the other religious communities that exist in the same town.

Nevertheless, a few liberal Christians have been actively generous in helping the newer communities to become settled and established. They have, for example, set up multi-faith committees in many areas, and they have experimented with multi-faith worship. There are even a few specialist 'multi-faith ministers', a remarkable new phenomenon. More concretely, Christians in the big cities have often been willing to give up their own surplus chapels to the incomers. This has involved a great deal of work in overcoming the fears of the outgoing Christians, and also of the local planning committees, about the conversion of a Christian building for use as a Hindu temple or a Sikh gurdwara.

These initiatives have been important, and it is worth recalling the original inspiration, which comes from biblical ideas about the end of history. The Israelite prophets looked for universal ethnic and religious reconciliation at the end of time, and liberal Christians see in many strands of modern history a partial fulfilment of that hope. We are indeed still struggling to create a peaceful and just international order; we are trying to create fully-reconciled multi-racial and multi-faith societies; and our great international humanitarian organisations are still battling to relieve suffering all over the world, without discriminating against anyone of whatever nation, race or creed. Modern Western emphasis on individual human rights, and especially modern feminism, are also part of Christianity's legacy to future generations.

I say all this because so many devout folk in all religions are apt to be suspicious of and hostile to modern Western culture, and the direction in which it is taking us all. I want to ask for a more discriminating analysis of modern secular culture, which will bring out the religious meaning of some of its achievements, and many of its best aspirations.

A number of other religions can make similar points: for example, the modern Western concern for animal welfare is less than 200 years old; but it has an ancient background in the teaching of Buddhists, Jains and Pythagoreans. And what I am asking for here – and also am proposing as Christianity's chief gift to our common future – is that we should all of us take a more hopeful and optimistic view of the modern world, and of our own prospects within it. Almost *all* religious people nowadays, of whatever faith, are tempted to see themselves as members of a beleaguered and declining minority group. We cling defensively to tradition, guard our ancient ways jealously, and see ourselves as threatened by enemies on every side. And this attitude becomes a self-fulfilling prophecy – by which I mean that if you see yourself as a member of a declining minority, then that is what you will be. If you have a victim psychology, then that psychology will tend to bring about the states of affairs that it fears. So I want to argue that we will all of us have a better future together if we can take a more discerning – and more optimistic – view of our cultural situation and prospects. Humankind will certainly have a religious future, and we can contribute to it – provided that we are willing to abandon our defensiveness and to accept change.

We need to give up the fears that inhibit us – and perhaps I should be specific here and say openly that we need to give up our fear of liberalism, of relativism and of humanism. Amongst conservative religious folk in every tradition these words are used as boo-words: they attract a knee-jerk reaction of hostility. But in fact modern liberalism, relativism and humanism are ultimately rooted in the very traditions that now react to them so suspiciously.

Take *liberalism*, for example. The Israelite prophet Hosea has a famous line that pictures God as declaring: 'I desire mercy, and not sacrifice'. St Matthew's Gospel has Jesus quoting it twice (Hosea 6:6; Matt 9:13, 12:7); and is it not the case that something to the same effect is said near the beginning of every great religious tradition? Morality is more important than ritual: love and compassion for one's fellow-humans are more important than the exclusivism and the hostility towards dissenters that religious groups so often display. And is not moral generosity and reluctance to condemn others a central tenet of liberalism?

Also characteristic of liberalism is the view that it is a mistake to see the religious realm as a special, distinct and protected sphere with its own special kinds of evidence and ways of thinking, a sphere within which criticism and questioning are out of place. Nowadays almost every traditional religious believer tries to keep her or his faith in a sealed-off area that is insulated from the ways of thinking that otherwise prevail everywhere in modern life. The liberals say that in the long run this is a mistake; and do not our faiths *themselves* tell us that the scope of religion, properly speaking, is as wide as the scope of human life itself?

We should not be afraid of liberalism, because its call to moral and intellectual truthfulness is a call which is also heard *within* our own faith-traditions.

Something similar can be said about *relativism*. Many people talk as if they think that the most authentic religious outlook is the most absolutist, by which they seem to mean that your doctrinal and moral principles, being revealed and eternal, should be held inflexibly, and without any regard to your cultural and historical situation. To which any lawyer, in any cultural tradition, will reply that if we are to live in accordance with general principles, whether of law or of faith or of morals, then we must apply them to particular cases – which means that we have to reckon with the detailed differences between different individuals, different cultures and different periods of history. Both in religion and in morality there always has to be *negotiation* between the general and the particular, between the ideal order and the changing world of actual human living. And again, this lesson is not one that we learn only from *outside* our own traditions, for it is also one that is taught *within* our traditions. We should not be afraid of relativism.

Thirdly, we should similarly not be afraid of modern Western *humanism*. It would be better for us to remember that a certain strain of humanism, and the image of a Cosmic Man, are found in almost all of our major religious traditions. Thus, in Judaism the biblical picture of 'man' as having been created in God's own image is developed by some of the rabbis into the doctrine of a cosmic Adam. This theme is further developed in early Christianity's classic image of the human Christ enthroned in majesty as ruler of the cosmos, and in the early Islamic doctrine of the Perfect Man, who is, says Rumi, 'the final cause of the world, being the epitome of God's desire to be known'. And this theme of the cosmic human being is familiar, not only in the Abrahamic or Middle-Eastern group of faiths, but also in the Indian group of faiths, where the theme of a Cosmic Giant or a Cosmic Buddha is prominent in the Hindu, Buddhist and Jain traditions.

Modern Western humanism is no doubt linked with the huge scope of modern 'man-made' knowledge, and the huge power of our modern technologies. We have, as it may be said, *appropriated* the whole world to ourselves and made it our own. Our knowledge and our technologies now shape every bit of it, and it is only *in our* knowledge and *in our* consciousness that the world becomes finished, bright, and *consciously* known and loved. Some see in this mighty process of world-appropriation a sinful modern human revolt against religion, but I suggest that we can and should see it as a partial fulfilment of a theme and a hope that is already announced – or at least, foreshadowed – in our ancient religious traditions. When Jesus was reported as saying that 'The Sabbath was made for man, and not man for the Sabbath' (Mark 2:27), he was reminding people that the religious concern is the concern for human *liberation*, not the concern for the repression and the control of human beings. Maybe it is true that many of our faiths look like, and are used as, instruments of social control and tools of power. When we see this, we should remind ourselves that there were once people for whom this faith was a revolutionary way to human emancipation.

Since I am now one of the old men myself, I hope I may be allowed to say that we should not be led astray by the elderly pessimists and nay-sayers who in every faith-tradition nowadays try to commit religion to being anti-liberal, anti-human and anti-life. It doesn't have to be like that. If we had all of us sufficient generosity of spirit, and perhaps a better knowledge of our own traditions, we could all of us take a much more optimistic view of humankind's religious future, and of the prospects for a multi-faith society here in Britain.

Believing and *Belonging* in a Pluralist Society – Exploring Resources in Islamic Traditions

Ataullah Siddiqui

'And indeed We have honoured the children of Adam...' Qur'an 17:70

'If your Lord so willed, He could have made mankind one people.' Qur'an 11:118

'O mankind, We have created you from a single (pair) of male and female and made you into nations and tribes that you may know each other.' Qur'an 49:13

Muslims are a faith-based community: *believing* and *belonging to* the community (the *ummah*) go hand in hand. By virtue of *belief* one *belongs to* and by virtue of *belonging* one *believes in*. Muslims in Britain know that they are living in a society which is not determined by religious affiliation, a society in which, while there are many religions, the relationship between the individual and any formal religion is often fluid. Further, many non-Muslim individuals with a concern for spirituality avoid linkages with formal religion and opt for a 'pick and mix' religion of their own choosing. Some acknowledge no religion at all and some might be described as 'illiterate' as far as religion is concerned. British Muslims cannot, however, live in isolation because the society in which they find themselves is an open society which demands participation. This paper seeks to explore some of the resources of Islam which will help to contribute to a religiously plural society.

The Qur'an is the anchor of the *believing* and *belonging* community and the Prophet Muhammad is its leader. The Qur'an is *about* human beings and is *for* human beings. Its earthly objective is to establish a cohesive, humane and just social order. The Qur'an aims to create a society where the individual and the society are under an obligation to 'enjoin good and forbid evil' (3:104; 110; 9:71). The Qur'an regards the Prophet Muhammad as one among many Prophets, some of whom it mentions while of others it says: 'We have not narrated to you ...' (40:78) but every people has been sent its guide (35:24). The Qur'an claims that, for every community, God has sent messengers and people will be 'judged between them with Justice, and they will not be wronged' (10:47). It also declares that for each community God has appointed a different path (*shir'ah*) and way (*minhaj*) (5:48). These different communities with various emphases of belief are encouraged to 'compete with one another (as in a race) in righteous deeds. Wherever you are God will bring you all together ...'(2:148).

Differences of belief are seen as part of God's plan. The abolition of such differences is not the purpose of the Qur'an, nor is the Prophet Muhammad sent for that purpose. The Qur'an also emphasises that such differences do not suggest that their origin is different, rather it emphasises that human beings have a common spirituality and morality (7:172, 91:7-10). The differences are there because God has given human beings the freedom to choose: 'If it had been your Lord's will, they would all have believed – all who are on earth! Will you then compel people against their wills to believe?' (10:99).

In this Qur'anic vision of unity and diversity the human task is to find a way to handle the differences. Issues should be discussed and debated so that consensus will be reached and no force be allowed to countenance aggression and violence (22:39-40). In all these processes Muslims are bound by their belief to co-operate with all – Muslims or not – in securing peace and justice. Even if that justice points to the guilt of one's family – let alone the community – the Qur'an instructs that justice must prevail (4:135).

These few verses from the Qur'an suggest that Muslims have enough theological resources to redefine their position in the contemporary world. A pluralist society can be built so that those involved, Muslim or otherwise, can feel free to engage and participate fully in the society that they are living in. And it is worth noting that the Qur'an claims itself as the book of Guidance (31:2-3). The Prophet Muhammad follows the Qur'an and shows the community what it means and how that should be practised. If a clear direction is not found in the Qur'an, Muslims are encouraged to look into the practices of the Prophet. If nothing is found there, the Muslim community – through its learned scholars – is encouraged to reach a consensus which is nearest to the spirit of Islam. In this process any attempt to freeze society in the norms of the past is not acceptable, nor is it tolerable to drag the society back to the past. What is required is to look back, keep the connection and not lose track. A keen eye is required to differentiate between what is *central* and what is *peripheral*.

Prophets throughout history, as the Qur'an points out, were born and brought up among the people to whom they preached. They always addressed them as their own people regardless of their belief. They were concerned about them and always wished the best for them. An important characteristic was that they reminded their people about their duty towards their Creator as well as their duty towards their fellow human beings. They pointed out their weaknesses and prophetically told them what would happen if they did not mend their ways. They always linked the need to worship One God and the need to stand on the side of justice. In other words, *believing* in God demands the duty of *belonging* to the community in a true sense. The Qur'an says, for example, 'And to Midian [a place north-east of the Sinai Peninsula] We sent forth their brother Shua'yb. He said to them: O my people! Serve God, you have no god but Him. Indeed a clear proof has come to you from your Lord. So give just weight and measure and diminish not to men their things and make no mischief on the earth after it has been set in good order' (7:85). Another example is Moses, who was sent to Pharaoh who oppressed and subjugated the children of Israel. Moses said, 'O Pharaoh! I am a messenger from the Lord of the Worlds, … to say nothing but truth … so let the Children of Israel depart along with me' (7:104-5).

These points suggest that, in an Islamic vision of a pluralist society, the mission of the Prophets includes all human beings, and justice and dignity are at its core. The Prophet Muhammad's mission was no different.

Though the city of Makkah at the time of the Prophet Muhammad was largely dominated by tribal loyalties, there were people who not only practised fairness and justice in their lives but also encouraged others to do so. An incident witnessed by the 20-year-old Muhammad took place in Makkah and helped the city to see through the haze of corruption and tribalism. A merchant from a foreign land (reports suggest he was from Yemen) arrived in Makkah and had dealings with a member of the influential Quraish tribe who received goods from the Yemeni trader but refused to pay for them. The Yemeni trader then pleaded with the leaders of the tribes and asked for justice. This incident became the immediate cause of the formation of an historic alliance of the tribes known as *Hil al-Fudul* ('Alliance of the virtuous' which was named after the three leading people whose name contained the word *fadl,* 'virtue', the singular of *fudul*). There was simmering discontent amongst the Makkans but they could do nothing because they lacked the necessary support from the tribal leaders.

The newly formed alliance immediately asked the Quraish man to pay the amount due to the Yemeni, which he did. The alliance also established the convention according to which a resident, or a stranger to the city, if treated unjustly would receive the full support of the members of the alliance and they would stand by the oppressed until justice had been done. The Prophet Muhammad was present when this historic alliance was made and remained loyal throughout his life to the convention. 'I would not exchange for the best of material gains', he said, 'if someone appeals to it in Islam I would respond.'

The last sentence is significant. Those people who participated in the alliance were not 'Muslims'. The Prophet's ministry was still 20 years away, yet in his Prophetic ministry he always remembered this alliance – conducted by 'non-Muslims' – with fond memory and strong approval. What it means is that anything that is commonly known as good (*ma'ruf*) should not wait for any religious approval or tag, rather it should be considered as part of one's own heritage. The Prophet once said that such a thing should be considered as a 'believer's lost property'.

Another landmark event took place when the Prophet migrated to Madinah. The first thing he did was to establish a Covenant between the *Ansars*, natives of Madinah, and the migrants from Makkah, the *Muhajirs*, who had left behind their businesses and property, and the Jews, the entrepreneurs of Madinan society. The Covenant was of great significance in that it was established against the backdrop of bloody and ruthless tribal conflicts. The document contained 52 sentences or 'clauses' and dealt with the concerns of those who had left their homes and had nowhere to live, and the concerns of those who, like the Jews, wanted their culture and norms to remain unchanged.[1] This document provided a basis for participation in the social life of the society. There was recognition that each party had a right to pursue its way of life and livelihood without encroaching upon others' rights and that each party had a duty to help and protect the other in times of crisis or of aggression from outside. It also recognised and established an acceptable pattern of compensation for the loss of life and property for all the people of Madinah. The Covenant was drafted after proper consultation with the leaders of the respective communities and consequently provided the kind of political system which was acceptable to all. It clearly stated that the 'God-fearing believers shall be against rebellions or him who seeks to spread injustice, or sin or enmity, or corruption between believers; the hand of every man shall be against him even if he be a son of one of them.'

Another incident in the Prophet's life indicative of his inclusiveness was shown in his relations with the ruler of Abyssinia, the Negus or Najashi, who was a Christian and known for his generosity and kindness. When the nascent Muslim community faced persecution in Makkah, the prophet encouraged his followers to take refuge in Abyssinia and the good qualities of the king were highlighted by the Prophet. Gradually, in small numbers, the Muslims began to arrive in Abyssinia and some of them interacted with the larger community and lived as a minority among the Christian majority. The Makkans however tried to win over the king with gifts and persuasion so that he would hand over to them these 'bandits' and 'culprits' of their society. The king refused but gave the refugees all the help they needed. However, another opportunity arose to persuade the king. Two years after the migration of the Prophet to Madinah the warlords of Makkah attacked Madinah but lost the battle. Fresh from defeat, they again asked the Negus to hand over the refugees who were still unable to join the Muslim community in Madinah. When the Prophet came to know about the intention of the Makkans he decided to send an envoy to Negus and chose 'Amar ibn Umaiyah ad-Damariy, a Christian.[2] It may be that this was political pragmatism and a pre-emptive action on the part of the Prophet but this does not diminish the fact that people who were not Muslims played a significant role in building a Muslim society. By their affiliation to other faiths they did not disqualify themselves from being part of a society where Islam was dominant.

The Negus died a few years after this incident. When the news reached the Prophet he told his companions that their brother had died, and that they should pray for him. He performed a special prayer which meant that the Negus died as a Muslim. But no one saw the Negus praying as a Muslim prays nor did he fast during the month of Ramadan as Muslims did. Throughout his life he remained a Christian and was known as generous and just. This incident suggests that we should not be judgmental about what is in the hearts of others and how God will judge a person for their belief. Salvation is not so crucial and central an issue in Islam as it is in Christianity. The central theme that runs throughout Islamic thought is to 'please God' and in that pleasure one finds solace and salvation. Furthermore this incident also suggests that our *belonging* has a much wider meaning than just to belong to our own community or *ummah*. In our humanity we connect with others. In the development of our own community we owe a great deal to others and, by their contribution to our community, in some way they too become part of us.

I would like to illustrate this point with another incident in the Prophet Muhammad's life: how this *belonging* has a wider connection.

The Makkans imposed a social boycott on Banu Hashim, the tribe that the Prophet belonged to. The Prophet's activities in Makkah were the main reason for this sanction. The Prophet's uncle, Abu Talib, was fearful that one day a mob might attack Muhammad and his few converts. He decided to take Banu Hashim to the safety of a valley where they remained for about three years. Nobody was allowed to sell food or to have business transactions of any kind with them. A number of elderly people and young children died of hunger and disease during this period. Such severe cruelty and injustice, where nobody was allowed to take even a small amount of food for the children in the valley, was opposed by people of dignity and decency, one of them being Mutim bin Adiy who consistently opposed the sanctions. He worked towards the cancellation of the decree of sanctions, a copy of which hung on the walls of the Ka'bah. He gained support from a few decent Makkan leaders and, eventually, he publicly tore down the decree.

Mutim bin Adiy also made another significant contribution, which stands out as a rare example of courage and fortitude. Concerned about the growing hostility towards the Prophet after the death of his uncle, Abu Talib, he went to the city of Ta'if to talk to the leaders of the influential *Taqif* family there. Though they listened to him they soon began to ridicule him and rejected his message of peace and justice. When the Prophet visited Ta'if they encouraged hooligans to deride the Prophet wherever he went. History records a bleeding Prophet, saying 'O God, to You I complain of my weakness, little resources and lowliness before men. O Most Merciful, You art the Lord of the weak and You art my Lord ... I take refuge in the light of Your countenance by which the darkness is illuminated. It is for You to be satisfied until You are well pleased. There is no power and no might save in You.' And he forgave his enemies.

The Prophet returned to Makkah. But according to the tradition of the time he had to 'renew' his 'stay' in Makkah and this was possible only if an influential family head would provide support. The Prophet approached the heads of various families through a mediator, seeking their support before he was allowed to enter Makkah. All turned him down, except Mutim bin Adiy who collected his weapons from his home, asked his sons and nephews to accompany him, escorted the Prophet to Makkah and declared that he was giving him the protection.

The message that emerges from such incidents is clear. Muslims in a pluralist society, particularly in today's context, need to re-examine their perceptions about the people around them. The tendency to perceive all non-Muslims as inherently 'antagonistic' to Islam and to Muslims and 'perpetually' conspiring against them, needs rethinking. There are very good souls and fine people beyond our own community.

Muslims have built their outlook on the basis of the Qur'an and the Prophetic traditions. They interpreted and contextualised Islam according to the world in which they found themselves. These interpretations and priorities always reflected the socio-political and economic conditions of the time. Soon after the Prophet's death, people's identity was based on their affiliation to their faith. A faith-based identity emerged and continued to provide a framework enabling all others to play a constructive role both within and also outside their communities. As far as Muslims were concerned, society's order and norms must be dictated by three elements: elimination of prejudice, easing hardship and establishing justice. These three elements are to be established in society irrespective of religious belonging. The elements should benefit the individual, and laws should be in place to protect these benefits and improve them according to time and place. In the Islamic tradition five basic necessities have been identified as essentials, as Al-Ghazali puts it, 'to promote the welfare of the people, which lies in safeguarding their faith, their life, their intellect, their posterity and their wealth. Whatever ensures the safeguarding of these five serves the public interest and is desirable.' The welfare of the individual and the community, as described by Ibn al-Qayyim, 'lies in complete justice, mercy, well-being and wisdom'. Anything that moves from welfare to misery has nothing at all to do with Islam. Ibn Taymiyyah further enhanced these objectives to include such things as the fulfilment of contracts, the preservation of ties of kinship and respect for the rights of one's neighbours. Today, Yusuf al-Qaradawi has argued to extend the list of the objectives to include human dignity, freedom, social welfare and human fraternity. [3]

In earlier times the Muslim world was largely divided between those who lived in Muslim territories (*Dar al-Islam*) and those who lived outside its domain, generally considered the territories of War (*Dar al-Harb*) but by 1839 the Tanzimat reforms in the Ottoman Caliphate changed the whole minority-majority concepts within and outside its boundary. The Tanzimat reform removed the faith-based identity and replaced it with citizenship.

The Ottoman Caliphate faced some difficulties in maintaining its role as a guardian of the Muslim *ummah,* on the one hand and, on the other hand, dealing with Muslims who were considered perhaps 'unreliable' because they lived in a territory which did not have any allegiance to the Caliphate. For example, a constant flow of Algerians began to leave their country after it was colonised by France which operated an aggressive Europeanisation policy that was resisted by the Algerians. Those who faced persecution in Algeria moved over time to Syria, which was under the Ottoman domain, and there they sought asylum but retained their French passports. They benefited both by being French, which allowed them to travel to France or Algeria, and by being Muslim if they wanted to live in the domain of the Caliphate. However, the situation became intolerable for the Ottomans and they required these asylum seekers to declare whether they regarded themselves as French or wanted to acquire Ottoman citizenship.

The Muslim subjects of Queen Victoria also posed a problem. Indian Muslims faced a dilemma when they arrived for *hajj* or pilgrimage in Makkah as, technically, they were considered travellers from an enemy territory but it was the duty of the Ottomans to receive and provide the necessary facilities for the pilgrims. A solution was found by the Ottomans in that they allowed the Indian Muslims to perform the pilgrimage and leave the Ottoman territory immediately after completing the rituals whereas other pilgrims from 'friendly' territories were allowed to stay for a longer period, even for months, in the holy land.[4]

Such events, and the increasing importance of the nation states where countries are dependent on migrant workers, have influenced the debate about faith-based identity in favour of citizenship as the basis of identity, but without denying the fellowship of the *ummah*.

Muslims' socio-religious discourse today is largely dominated by the discourse of Muslims living in a predominantly Muslim society. Muslim jurisprudence and its legacy are largely an exploration of how Muslims ruled and conducted their affairs within and with the outside world. They do discuss minorities but within their domain. It is a rich and excellent source. Those living as a significant minority for centuries are almost lost in this discourse. In Cyprus, for example, Muslims lived as a minority and Muslim rulers and Cypriots concluded a treaty in the 7th century whereby Cyprus remained outside the domain of the Muslim Caliphate for centuries. Muslims lived there and conducted their affairs in peace and harmony. But how did they live there? And how did they conduct their affairs in the midst of a Christian majority? How did they maintain their identity as Muslims and at the same time feel at ease living there? Over the centuries, and particularly during the last hundred years or so, Muslim discourse has been led by political priorities and has had little opportunity to explore the issues of jurisprudence and theology and the challenges faced by significant Muslim populations. The recent mass migration of Muslims to Europe and North America is forcing Muslims to revisit their theological roots and reconnect them with today's world. There is an urgency to search for a new language that will be recognisably Islamic and will have regard not only to those Muslims living as minorities but also those minorities of other faiths who are living amongst Muslim majorities. *Believing* demands that our relationship with God be strengthened but it also demands that our communal *belonging* should not be conducted in isolation from all other communities.

Bibliography

1. See the full text, translation and a short commentary by Muhammad Hamidullah, *The First Written Constitution in the World: An Important*

Document of the Time of the Holy Prophet, (3rd revised ed), Sh Muhammed Ashraf, Lahore, 1975.

2. Muhammad Hamidullah, *The Muslim Conduct of State*, (revised ed) Sh Muhammad Ashraf, 1977, p 205.
3. See for details M Hashim Kamali, 'Maqasid Al-Sharia: The Objectives of Islamic Law', Newsletter of the Association of Muslim Lawyers and the Islamic Foundation's Legal Studies Unit, Vol 3 Issue 1 (April-June 1998), pp13-19.
4. Deringli, Selin, *The Well-Protected Domains*, London, IB Tauris, 1998, pp 55f.

Hinduism as 'the eternal philosophy'

David A Hart

> *They have called him Indra, Mitra, Varuna, Agni,*
> *And the divine fine-winged Garuda;*
> *They spoke of Indra, Yama, Matrarisvan:*
> *The One Being sages call by many names.*   Rig Veda 1: 164: 46

Of the seven major religious traditions considered in this book, the Hindu faith is the most difficult to define and thereby to handle. Judaism focuses on the law given to Moses and Christianity speaks of Jesus of Nazareth as the Christ. Islam is the Koranic revelation to Mohammed and Buddhism focuses on the life and message of Gautama Siddharta. Sikhism came out of a clearly defined area of north-west India and was related to a specific collection of gurus, and Bahai came out of 19th-century Persia and focused on the teachings of Baha-u-llah.

But of Hinduism it is difficult indeed to define its main area and its focus of teachings and status. Let us examine each of these three areas of definition to reveal the areas of contention. India is not a well-defined piece of land, indeed, its interconnectedness with Asia has even denied it full status as a continent, so that it is usually referred to as a 'sub-continent' without it being deemed necessary (in colonial times) to specify who or what it was 'under'!

Most authorities point to the Indus river, flowing from the Himalayas to the Arabian Sea in the north-west of India, as the source of the term, found in a Persian form as *Sindhu* in what is perhaps the oldest portion of the Vedas, the Rig Samhita, dated around 1200-1000 BCE. The area in consideration was always a trade route and terrain of mobile populations, making it difficult to view these geographical origins as of a rooted people. Towards the beginning of the first millennium BCE the fair-skinned Aryans, who came from the western regions beyond the passes and adopted Sanskrit for language, began to dominate the area. A little later, towards the middle of the first millennium, the Persians, under Darius I, began to come down into the territory from the north. So a European origin for a population on the move downwards into India provided the cradle for this religion and its culture to develop.

Further down south were the darker, Dravidian cultures with their separate languages and cults. Successive waves of empire, Moghul and British, swept down from the north but in fact made little impact on the southernmost extremes of the subcontinent, to such an extent that the British allowed the maharajahs of Travancore to continue their rule without any specific adjustments to the rule of the Raj. Particular southern cults and deities, primarily that of the goddess Kali, common also to the island of Sri Lankha, continued to flourish. When the categorisation of indigenous religions began in the academies of Germany, Holland and Britain in the 18th century, it proved a category too easy to resist, to call all non-monotheistic cults encountered 'Hinduism', though the valuation of it as a religious phenomenon vacillated immensely from 'enlightened pagan' to 'diabolical'.

At the other end of the timescale, during the last century and a half there has been a vast emigration from India to many other continents so there are distinct and sizeable Hindu communities in the Middle East, Europe, Africa, North America, and Australasia. In these communities, inter-caste and interfaith marriages in vast numbers have rendered the concept of a distinctive Indian 'race' highly problematic. Coinciding with these emigrations have been conscious missionary endeavours by groups wishing to spread the 'eternal philosophy' outside the Indian subcontinent. So Vivekenanda's visit to Chicago to speak to the World Parliament of Religions in 1893 was followed by his founding the Ramakrishna Mission Association to spread the universal teachings of his guru Sri Ramakrishna (1836-1886) and in 1899 he returned to the USA and founded the Vedanta Society of California. About the same time, Rammohan Roy founded the Brahmo Samaj to support inclusive Hindu respect for the person of Jesus and his ethical teachings. Also, Prabhupada took a form of universal Hinduism to Australia and California when he founded the International Society for Krishna Consciousness. His teachings were influential in turn on the young writer Christopher Isherwood who introduced many of the concepts of Hinduism to the generation of post-war British poets and radical writers.

It is worth noting how the influence of some of these international movements feeds back into Hindu self-understandings in the motherland. For example, although entry into temples in the south-east state of Tamilnadu has always been permitted, non-Hindus are generally not allowed to enter the temples of the south-west state of Kerala. However, in a number of these temples in recent years possession of a certificate from Bhaktivedanta Manor (British headquarters of the Hare Krishna Movement) has been the sole requirement for a British visitor to prove her Hindu identity!

If we prefer to define Hinduism by its teachings, we face further problems of circumscription, due to the diversity of the *sruti* or 'written scriptures' that can be appealed to. The relationship between the earliest Vedas, the Upanishads, the Brahma Sutra, the Bhagavad-gita, the Ramayana and the Mahabharata is complex, with many inter-textual relationships both grammatical and theological. If the primitiveness of the Vedas is deemed to give them special authority, their arcane subject matter (one entirely about horse-sacrifice!) and poetic language detract from their usefulness as defining indicators of tradition. In some ways the most popular and cherished religious text (analogous to the Bible) could well be the Gita, so it might be illuminating to spend a little time examining its presuppositions and prescriptions about Hindu religion.

Firstly, its setting is in those plains of north-west India but in a mythic time, when general Arjuna drives his horses into battle and communes with the divine Krishna who takes the form of his chariot-driver for the purpose of the dialogue. The central question is whether Arjuna should fight or not, specially because if he decides to, he will likely end up killing a number of his family members since it's an internecine war and a lot of them are on the enemy's side. On the other hand, if he fails to fight the dispute will remain unsettled and drag on without resolution. This is the basic dilemma of the ruler of a large country and well illustrated in the life of Emperor Asoka.

The basic discourse that ensues between Arjuna and Krishna is thus one of action and the causes of action, and in the course of that dialogue the distinctive Hindu teaching on *karma* is elucidated as the ineluctable law of cause and effect. This law is described as an eternal law that is embedded within the nature of things – it is not specific to a particular culture, place or religion. As a law it is universally operative and applicable to anyone regardless of his or her faith. Basically, the law teaches that one reaps what one sows both in the physical and in the spiritual world, so that a life of altruism and caring for others will inevitably free the individual from the bonds of selfishness, while someone who is always grasping and acquiring for herself will not be able to be freed from the desires of avarice. Thus far the theory is framed philosophically (way of *jnana*) but when it is cast in more specifically religious terms (way of *bhakti*) this idea becomes expressed in universal terms that are quasi-monotheistic, and are therefore extremely open to our multi-faith interpretation:

> I am the father of this universe, the mother, the support, and the grandsire. I am the object of knowledge, the purifier and the syllable om. I am also the Rig, the Sama, and the Vedas. I am the goal, the sustainer, the master, the witness, the abode, the refuge and the most dear friend. I am the creation and the annihilation, the basis of everything, the resting place and the eternal seed.

> But those who worship Me with devotion, meditating on My transcendental form – to them I carry what they lack and preserve what they have. Whatever a man may sacrifice to other gods, O son of Kunti, is really meant for Me alone, but it is offered without true understanding.

> 9: 17f, 22f (in Prabhupada's 1972 translation)

It is within the Bhagavad-gita that we also find Krishna voicing a justification for the four-fold system of stratification of humanity according to function, which gives Hinduism its distinctive understanding of caste, which many take to be essential to the system. Topping and controlling this system, the Brahmin caste rule unopposed by their arcane ritual knowledge and their skills in the subtleties of the Sanskrit language, passed on from generation to generation within elite schools. Although the significance of such social stratification within the religion and society can scarcely be denied in Hindu history, two points can be made which would lead us to a more inclusive understanding of the system. The first is pointed out by many commentators on the Gita: that as Arjuna described the division on the basis of function in a section on human work and its importance, the very functionalism of the system suggests that it has a pragmatic rather than an ideological base. The true Brahmin is thus not so much one who undergoes the ceremony of the sacred thread as the one who articulates and upholds the universal law of *karma*. Also, since the time of Gandhi modern Hindus seem to have been embarrassed by this cultural legacy and wished to move away from a rigorous classification of caste which excludes significant percentages of the population from access to social and religious practice. The outlawing of caste in the Indian Constitution and the system of Dalit Quotas introduced after Independence and maintained even by the BJP Government shows that this significant factor in the history of Hinduism can scarcely be defined as a building block.

A society of a billion plus population needs leadership and a sense of stratified social responsibilities, and in this regard the concept of 'caste' maintains some of the ambivalence given to 'class' in British society. The line of the government and the more enlightened sections of the society suggest that it scarcely exists and is far less important than previously, while sociological analyses reveal that the system is as undergirding as ever, even if allowing more flexibilities into its workings as the result of an inevitable underlying pluralism within the social fabric of 21st-century life.

In his excellent *An Introduction to Hinduism* (Cambridge University

Press 1996) Gavin Flood points out that there is a tension in the religion today between global Hinduism and political nationalism because of the perceived connection between the Hindu Dharma and Bharat, the nation-state of India.

The litmus test for Hinduism is how it appears in practice. It has had the advantage of being a faith born in a country that was cradle to half a dozen religions, and so co-existence has been a *sine qua non* of the faith from its earliest years. As one of the oldest religions, it may well have instigated many of the beliefs and practices we find also in other faiths. It has also shown itself able, sponge-like, to soak up many of the practices of other faiths. This is very well illustrated historically in the life and thought of one of the greatest of India's emperors, the founder of the Moghul dynasty, Akbar (1542-1605). By birth a Muslim, Akbar married a Hindu wife and hired a Christian tutor. As a result of their and other influences in North India (including Buddhism and Jainism), Akbar formulated a court code Tawhid-I-Ilahi ('Divine Unity Principle') in which a multi-faith amalgam is presented as a viable faith.

Where Hinduism has moved outside India, it has shown itself very able to adapt to other ideas and lifestyles. Thus, for example, in Mauritius where Hindus constitute half the population, love-marriages seem to have replaced arranged marriages leading to a practical abolition of caste, while in Britain worship in temples appears to have focused on Sundays, adopting Christian practice, and Hindu pundits appear to have adopted many of the pastoral habits of the Christian clergy, including pastoral visiting and institutional chaplaincies. Even in India, you are as likely to see Jesus or the Virgin Mary as an image on the wall of a temple as the Indian figures Sai Baba or the Sikh Guru Nanak. A pantheon of gods and goddesses seems a good starting point for a faith open to a variety of theological interpretations, and an emphasis on religious practice rather than dogma enables Hindus to navigate their way with considerable aplomb and enthusiasm in a culture that has just recently turned as consciously pluralistic as Britain in the 21st century.

Cross-Cultural Dialogues with Western Fictions: 'there is neither Hindu nor Muslim' … nor Sikh[1]

Balbinder Singh Bhogal

naa ko hinduu hai naa ko musalaaman.
There is neither Hindu nor Muslim.
Guru Naanak (Puraatan Janam-saakhii)

beda katebii bhedu na jaataa.
Neither the Vedas nor the Islamic scriptures know the Mystery.
Guru Naanak (AG:1021, Maaruu Solahe 2, 6:1)[2]

naam thaam na jaati jaakara ruup ranga na rekha.
aadi purakha udaara muurati ajoni aadi asekha.
desa aur na bhesa jaakara ruupa rekha na raga …
Without name, place or caste, without form, colour or mark.
Primal Being, Benevolent Form, Unborn, Primal, Infinite.
Confined to no country or garb, to no form, mark or attachment …
Guru Gobind Singh (Jaap, v 80)

The concept of a multi-faith Britain demands, or even presupposes, a substantial discourse on inter-religious dialogue. However such discourse has tended to assume that such a dialogue can only occur if one focuses on the similarities rather than the obvious differences, and this bias is thereafter held as a universal truth, to cite one recent Sikh example from Indarjit Singh:

> … the actual teachings of the world's major religions are remarkably similar … [However] recognition of this universal truth … does not mean that there are no important differences of belief and emphasis, but it does mean that our different faiths have much more in common than the 'leaders' of religion would sometimes have us believe … the areas in common are far greater than the differences. [3]

The usual argument implies that religious differences are seen as reasons for discrimination and are therefore negative; if only we could see our similarities we would not need to fight. However, such an assumption is wholly unsubstantiated: when it comes to the details people simply cannot agree upon what those similarities are or indeed what they should be. Take each religion and see the often vehemently opposed interpretations of one book, one doctrine and one creed. Rather, it would seem that 'peace and understanding' could only arise out of an intelligent respect for another's difference. Indarjit Singh's intolerance of difference is a naïve and dangerous misreading of social reality. If anything, inter-religious dialogue should cultivate an intelligence that can tolerate and engage with difference, rather than pretend that differences are negligible, or that only a certain (liberal, Western, elite) cluster of 'similarities' represents the 'civilised' world and its values, which 'all' 'religions' happen to share. Indeed, others have argued that the appeal for a common denominator around and upon which all discussion can occur is wholly misguided. [4] How then to view difference differently, positively? How to base dialogue on difference rather than appeals to romanticised similarities? How to view the other with equal respect? How to hear the other's voice as a challenge? How not to be threatened by differences, and how not to be comforted by similarities?

This chapter will focus on inter-religious dialogue, the appointed overseer of a multi-faith Britain. But we need to ask whether it is always 'good to talk'. Would not one be a fool to enter into a dialogue with a fool, for example? Indeed Guru Naanak (the 'founder' of the 'Sikh religion') does not hesitate to reply:

> *muurakha gandhu pavai muhi maara.*
> (The only way) to establish a relation with a fool is to strike him on his mouth.
>
> Guru Naanak (AG:143, *Raagu Maajha* 2, 12: *paurii* 12)

Naanak's 'politically incorrect' rough realism resists a sanitised, elite discourse that may soon disappear into its dialogical hubris, leaving in its wake another repetition of the Imperial Same. As the opening quotations suggest, the Sikh point of departure should be clear: there is no special language (Sanskrit, Arabic, Guramukhi), nor people (Hindu, Muslim, Sikh), nor scripture (Vedas, Qu'ran, Adi Granth), nor place (Mecca, Harimandir Sahib, Khalistan) that can claim the mystery as captured, interpreted and/or explained: truth is unspeakable even when it is spoken; prophets speak but are differently heard.

The construction of 'world religions' as the basis of inter-religious dialogue

It is obvious to most that the West can no longer see itself as the centre of the world with all else at its periphery; the 'margins' are now being recognised as centres in their own right. The 'West and the rest' is a phrase that captures the disrespect and imperial myopia of a time now fading from contemporary memory. The present is now perceived to be polycentric and each centre has itself become also a margin, identity is double, shifting, Ricoeur's 'I as another' – or so the rhetoric goes. Yet the globalisation of a largely Euro-American culture, via ruthless capitalist consumer markets and multinational corporations, reveals the real inequalities of power each centre actually wields. Every discourse is therefore skewed by such hegemonic, economic and informatic power 'vectors' in their cross-cultural transfer and representation. It is hard to uphold the notion of an innocent dialogue, where dialogue is not distorted by the propaganda of more powerful centres of control, be they political, religious or socio-economic. Just as there can be no innocent retrieval of the past, so is there no innocent reading of the present. It is not the case that traditions were once pure and now have become corrupted, but more the case that heterogeneity is the beginning, and its ceaselessly weaving patterns a constant.

While Tracy is right in detecting a 'new prophetic call to a dialogical and polycentric theology',[5] his over-determination of this dialogical space by semitic, and particularly Christian, terminology can only skew the debate to repeat its imperial and colonial past. King, at the recent conference on *Dialogue and Difference*, offered a critique of the

post-Enlightenment notions of 'interfaith dialogue' on the grounds
that they are 'Eurocentric in their orientation, ambitions and cultural
exchange'. [6] More specifically with respect to the construction of
'world religions', Gonçalves notes that:

> current tendencies to represent religions as autonomous worlds of praxis
> and discourse exemplify an unjustified reification of identity – a reification
> which is not only ahistorical and inadequate to the phenomena being
> theorized, but which both implicitly and explicitly serves to further the
> interests of those committed to essentialist interpretations of their own
> traditions in the pursuit of allegedly orthodox authenticity. [7]

The colonially inspired constructions of 'Hinduism' and 'Sikhism' as
coded and often internally consistent systems may well form the very
obstacles to dialogue, as Naanak was himself so obviously aware. To
the extent to which inter-religious dialogue is committed to operate
at the level of 'world religions', it becomes a discourse about
theoretical phantoms. It is interesting to note here, within the context
of a professed 'dialogue with the other', that, 'such reification allows
the theorisation of hybridity and transformation only in terms of
heterodox deviation or alien contamination'. [8] An identity in the
abstract can assume a level of purity and non-self-contradiction that
simply does not exist in the real complex world of interwoven
religiosities and translated identities. It is only at the level of theorised
discourse that 'alien invaders' and 'deviants' can be clearly identified.
To the extent to which inter-religious dialogue operates within these
categories and homogenised identities, the debate becomes a red
herring, though one not without its religio-political consequences.
Books that seek to 'cover' the 'major world religions' speak as much,
if not more, about the academic discipline and its theorisation and
categorisation of 'religion' and 'dialogue' as they do about their
subject matters and the process of engaging in a dialogue with 'the
other'.

However, this problem of cross-cultural translation, of
oversimplifying the passage from one socio-linguistic culture to
another, even occurs within the same traditions across time. Tracy is
therefore right to ask, 'is the Christian narrative Christendom or

Christianity?', [9] thus highlighting the selective and problematic readings and retrievals of past heritage. Likewise Sikhs need to ask whether the Sikh narrative is *Khalistan* (the fight for an independent Sikh state) or *guramati* (teachings of the Gurus as given in the AG), the living Sant-guru (contemporary human gurus), or the Khalsa/Satiguru (True-Guru). [10] Are the two mutually exclusive? Can one even speak about the 'Christian' or 'Buddhist' view? The notion of 'inter-religious dialogue' is in important senses mere fantasy because it is based on wholly unreal homogenised totalisations: 'Christianity', 'Hinduism', 'Buddhism' do not exist in themselves but there are many 'Christian', 'Hindu' and 'Buddhist' traditions. [11]

Taking the 'world religions' as a stage for inter-religious dialogue seems only to lead to a theatrical debate, one that must be seen to be happening by Western liberals. Such constructed performances work on a monocultural and monological basis seeking to mirror an 'ideal dialogue'. This orientation ignores the localisations and problems of how knowledge is formed, re-presented and disseminated. For example Kuhn's paradigms, Wittgenstein's language games, Lyotard's metanarratives, and Foucault's epistemes all historicise and contextualise the presuppositions that lie behind any knowledge base. More to the point of cross-cultural dialogues, issues of power and knowledge (Foucault), gender (Irigrary, Kristeva, Harding) and colonialism (Said, Spivak, Bhabha), are all too easily side-stepped by the liberal inclusivist and pluralist agendas.

Inter-religious dialogue too often concerns the constructed macro-identities at the expense of changing interpretations at the micro or individual/sect level. The socio-political movements that have vested interests in the contemporary constructions of their own traditions take precedence over the religious writings of those very traditions. In other words, too rigid a focus on 'Christianity' will destroy dialogue with the Bible; likewise too fervent a devotion to 'Islam' will stifle a contemporary 'dialogue' with the Qu'ran; too adamant an adherence to 'Sikhism', or the orthodox view, will simply silence a possible dialogue with the Guru Granth Sahib – especially, and ironically, when these religions claim a universal and timeless import to their teachings.

The construction of such totalised units that can stand, supposedly, the test of time, denies that those very interpretations are inextricably tied to an historical, political and translative process, which each generation grapples with. Simply relying on the erroneous assumption that a particular revelation 'speaks itself' to all people throughout time is to ignore the diversity of traditions, languages and types of revealed writings, as well as the whole notion of dialogue – between self and other, both personally and publicly, diachronically and synchronically. This fundamentalist reading of revelation suppresses what always accompanies dialogue and dissemination: the complexity of cross-cultural translation. Understanding inter-religious dialogue as cross-cultural translation will inevitably involve a consideration of its relation to European colonisations, and their complicity with missionary activity and orientalist monologues of anthropology.

Inter-religious dialogue as present-day analogue of anthropology

> But the ethnographer has not only to spread his nets at the right place, and wait for what will fall into them. He must be an active huntsman, and drive his quarry into them and follow it up to its most inaccessible lairs. [12]

Even the word 'dialogue' requires serious contextualisation: for cultures beyond the 'West' have different notions of communication, thus what is meant by 'dialogue' is certainly not universal and obvious. Is the motivation for inter-religious dialogue stained by this superior, imperial, elite-educated huntsman?

The trajectory of inter-religious dialogue, as a professional and institutionalised pursuit, can be traced back to 19th-century anthropology. [13] Inter-religious dialogue is tied to colonially-inspired ethnographic monologues, for the West is still setting the agenda and still asking the question 'who are you?', 'what do you believe?', 'what use are you to us?', 'what do you have to contribute or say for yourself?', and more concisely in the imperative 'Explain yourself!'. A monologue about difference is a mode of discourse that masks one's own (religious, imperial) speech as untranslatable – ie as superior, unquestionable, whether this is a conscious move or not. While Europe's past is studied historically and its present analysed by social science, it is never studied anthropologically. It is only the non-European other, that is approached via anthropology, for 'that is a discipline designed to help "us" understand "them"'. [14]

Ethnographic *writing* (or the informant's report) – hardly a dialogical medium in itself – is institutionally and historically monological. This scribal transformation of native knowing and being by the anthropologist formed a monolithic orientalist archive that 'enlightened' imperial discourse in terms of better rulership and governance. [15] Not only is the mode of translation heavily skewed and biased towards the Western observer, the power dynamics of early evolutionary theories, where perfect Christianity would be the goal that all other religions were developing towards, have meant that inter-religious dialogue has gained its trajectory from a misguided monologue of the other, that speaks more about its own dark side than the other's difference, and has yet to check itself, to silence its propelling desire. [16]

> The ethnographic encounter is never a symmetrical relation ... in most cases, the ethnographer comes as an uninvited guest. Why should the natives meet and talk to him at all? ... In colonial times, the native could still be compelled into the ethnographic encounter by pure violence. Emile Nolde for example, a German painter who visited New Guinea at the beginning of the century, used to put his pistol near his right hand when he painted portraits of the natives to prevent them from escape. [17]

The coloniser/colonised relation is grafted upon the Western ethnographer and the 'native other'. And it is these relations that predispose current inter-religious dialogues.

> As a rule, the goal of the one who opens dialogue is to convince his interlocutor of the validity of his own arguments. Or have you ever seen a Christian church leader who decided to become a Muslim after one of these so often pled for inter-religious dialogues with Islam? [18]

There is then the bitter taste of guilt at the root/route of the inter-religious dialogical demand – not only because it is commanded, but also because the ground rules upon which this debate can and 'only' operate are discovered and established by the 'West': the 'dialogue' occurs in English, is framed by Western agendas and categories, assumes the Western construction of 'world religions' as normative, and is desired by the West. For example, Swidler's 'dialogue decalogue' with its awful mimesis of revelation and historical imperial order in his 'ten commandments of dialogue' provides us with yet another example of the theoretical speculations of a liberal elite setting the agenda and prescribing 'the way ahead' for all. [19]

How can Christian (sacred and secular) traditions enter a 'dialogue' with the 'other' beyond the trope of conversion and without erasing their own claims of 'absolute truth'? The doctrinal-missionary and colonial-scientific histories of the Christian West conspire against inter-religious and intercultural dialogue, and leave only a monological drive.

Inter-religious dialogue, since its discourse has largely *not* been affected by the other's words and worldview, is actually only an a-visceral Western dilemma that has little or minimal relation to the real world composed of different people, places, languages, values and cultures. The politics of difference does not bite into the eel of inter-religious monologue, a monologue which does not heed the emergence of a new polycentric world and its real challenge even in its very attempt to come face to face with the other. The Euro-American centre has to become a margin to the many centres it has for too long ignored and spoken for, and wait there, listening to, and learning from, different voices and orderings of Being – if they happen to be communicated to them. As Tracy notes, 'If it [the West] clings to its former senses of being the center, this center cannot heal itself.'[20]

> *To be means to communicate.* Absolute death (non-being) is the state of being unheard, unrecognized. [21]

Inter-religious dialogue as cross-cultural translation (of the untranslatable)

> Translation thus produces strategies of containment. By employing certain modes of representing the other – which it thereby also brings into being

– translation reinforces hegemonic versions of the colonized ... [these representations, or Said's 'objects without history'] become *facts* exerting a force on events in the colony: witness Thomas Babington Macaulay's 1835 dismissal of indigenous Indian learning as outdated and irrelevant, which prepared the way for the introduction of English education. [22]

When translation is the handmaiden of colonialism, it becomes instrumentalised and enmeshed within a range of cultural stereotypes ordered in favour of the rulers. In the political sphere translation becomes propaganda. In the scholarly arena there has been a scientific pretence that the re-presentation of 'other' people, their works and events, in another socio-linguistic culture can occur without too much distortion, if any! However such notions of translation and the concepts and categories that are created and employed, 'completely occlude the violence that accompanies the construction of the colonial subject'. [23] Inter-religious dialogue has for too long ignored its own politics of cross-cultural translation, especially in employing categories that have become static and unchanging, fixed as abstractions of an elite discourse. Naming the other as 'Hindu' or 'Sikh', as followers of only 'one' 'religion', *either* 'Hinduism' *or* Sikhism', relates a colonial, ethnographically informed, discourse that bears little resemblance to reality and has no cognisance of the historical constructedness of these distinct categories within a politically charged arena. Dialogue is not only about representing or understanding the other, but also translating and transforming the other. In fact it becomes difficult to avoid the following rubric: dialogue is translation, translation is understanding, and understanding is always already framed by a kaleidoscope of historically situated interpretations and appropriations. [24]

Inter-religious dialogue is in fact cross-cultural translation, and as such those who enter dialogue are also entering the realm of translation, viz, transformation. Indeed if all conversations are predisposed on reciprocal exchange, then in listening to the other, one may be dramatically affected by that other and vice versa. This seems to suggest that there is no dialogue between two fixed identities. That would rather be a recipe for war. Dialogue is therefore not about the fixity of two, but more about a particular engagement that undoes and reconstructs selves in relation. Bakhtin notes, 'Truth is not born nor is it to be found inside the head of an individual person, it is born *between* people collectively searching for truth, in the process of their dialogic interaction'. [25] Truth, it would seem, is an intersubjective endeavour, not a search for the Final or Ultimate Word disclosed only to a favoured people, in a special language and place – that is the discourse of a centre that has forgotten that itself is formed by the other whether in opposition or synthesis. If thinking itself requires dialogue, then selfhood is better understood as intersubjective 'I-Other'.

Silence within speech: a plea of a silent dialogue

cupai cangaa naanakaa vinu navai muhi gandhu.
To be silent is good, O Naanak, without the Name (the words of) the mouth produce a stench.
  Guru Naanak (AG:1288, *Malaara-kii-vaara, paurii* 23, *saloku* 1: 4)

Language coupled with the notion of dialogue can so easily render silence silent, absent. However, behind speech, silence unravels all discourse: silence cannot be silent. There seems to be an 'unbearable absence every word butts up against, as any given name does against the unpronounceable divine Name'. [26] If silence is 'not merely the contrary of language', [27] to avoid simply making a 'noise', inter-religious dialogue should aim first to become silent and cultivate a listening to oneself as another, and only then attempt to speak silence. This would, however, require a difficult language of self-transformative humility where each party allows themselves to become translated into the other's words, with due circumspection. Even 'revelation' denies absolute interpretation across time since it demands its perpetual interpretation in one's daily life and language. Representatives of various religious traditions should not forget the silence that scriptural revelations speak in their formulations of what they supposedly say. In speaking we are only ever communicating silence, our inability to speak the absolute beyond our language.

The beginning of dialogue (its listening) is always the cessation of dialogue (its talking), whether perceived or not. 'Dialogue' gives the impression of movement, whereas it is a cyclical meditational return to the unsaid in all that is said. Dialogue is therefore another word for unravelling all speech that forgets its metaphorical (and so arbitrary) origin. The call for dialogue is always a forgetting (of our inability to force silence to speak). Speech is always riddled with the silence of untranslatability; when the unspeakable is spoken, it is not as one and the same, but the same and different, I and other:

> *eka mahi saraba saraba mahi ekaa eha satiguri dekhi dhikhaaii.*
> All are within the One and the One is within all, this vision the True-Guru has shown me.
>   Guru Naanak (AG: 908, *Raamakalii, asatapadiiaa*, 8, 5: 1)

When a self or a group loses its relation to otherness as constitutive of its own self, then it becomes sick, a shadow and a repetition that has lost its temporal nature eschewing an ethical space. Speech becomes literally about oneself. However, from Guru Naanak's view, there is a speaking beyond oneself, with the noise of the ego dismantled, for some speak silence:

> *jiu bolaae tiu boliiai jaa aapi bulaae soi.*
> As He causes me to speak, so do I speak, when He Himself causes me to speak.
>   Guru Amardas (AG: 39, *Srii Raagu*, 63, 30, 4: 1)

The monological overdrive of ego-speech only reveals a distaste for dialogue and the inevitability of being answerable to the other through a real communication. In other words, without listening all one's speech becomes a monologue of deafness/unhearing endlessly regurgitating and disseminating the repetition of the 'same-tired-old-truths'. But, for Naanak, it is a crucial first step to cultivate a closeness to silence and the ability to listen; not only dialogue depends upon it but also communion, and spiritual power:

> *suniai satu samtokhu giaanu …*
> *suniai andhe paavahi raahu.*

By listening truth, contentment and (divine) knowledge [is obtained] ...
By listening [even] the blind find the way.

Guru Naanak (AG: 3, Japu, 10: 1; 11: 3)

For Guru Naanak, the only dialogue worth engaging with is one where speech occurs without speaking. True speech, for Guru Naanak, is non-dual, paradoxical and ungraspable:

bakai na bolai hari guna gaavai. . .
Without uttering or saying a word, one should sing Hari's [God's] praises
...

Guru Naanak (AG: 411, Aasaa, asatapadiiaa, 1, 1: 2)

There is then dualistic dialogue and nondualistic dialogue; to speak meaningfully about the 'real', one has to speak without speaking, describe without describing, act without acting:

akhii baajhahu vekhanaa vinu kannaa sunanaa.
pairaa baajhahu calanaa vinu hathaa karanaa.
jiibhai baajhahu bolanaa iu jiivata maranaa.
naanaka hukamu pachaani kai tau khasamai milanaa.
(Who is) seeing without eyes, hearing without ears,
walking without feet, working without hands,
speaking without tongue and thus dying while living:
(He), (says) Naanak, having known the Divine Order, is then united with the Lord.

Guru Angad (AG: 139, Maajha-kii-vaara, sa 1)

Words owe their strength less to the certainty of their articulation than to the lack, the abyss, the inventive uncertainty in what they say. [28]

Muslims, Hindus and Sikhs (et al) must think beyond simply being 'Muslim', 'Hindu' or 'Sikh' – as Guru Naanak urges, otherwise they will only produce monological noise in their 'dialogues'. The inability to think beyond powerful practices and discourses of inscription (national, racial, ideological, religious, gender, class, caste, etc) leads to the framing of otherness as dualistic, and so only combative. Muslims, Hindus, and Sikhs have first to learn how to listen and talk to the various marginalised 'sects' and groups within their own traditions before they can converse across religions. Inter-religious dialogue must wait for the healing that must arise out of an *intra-religious* dialogue. That is to say, inter-religious dialogue must move beyond dialogue as apologetics towards dialogue as translation, from dialogue as self and tradition to dialogue as self-other and tradition-in-transition, from egoistic dialogue as noise, to selfless dialogue as silence.

The inter-religious monologue that wears the Emperor's clothes of dialogue is an art of elite, liberal self-deception. If one does not analyse the shadows of one's own 'dialogue', ie that which configures, informs, predisposes it, then one's speech-act will be destined to repeat, abstract and so alienate itself and others. Dialogue here is a monological discourse of unhearing that silences through stating the said as power. One can only accept it or live the political consequences of its denial. The inter-religious monologue, disguised as dialogue, represents a failure to see the Emperor's new clothes as phantoms of collective delusion. Rather, dialogue is about listening to, and hearing the irresolvable silence of Otherness speak to itself through oneself and the world.

References

1. I would like to thank Sophie Hawkins for reading the final draft of this chapter and making many sound suggestions, as well as corrections.
2. The Guru Granth Saahib will be abbreviated as AG (Adi Granth, 'First Book'), its name given on its compilation by the fifth Guru in 1604.
3. Indarjit Singh, 'If you're wearing a turban you must be a terrorist', *Independent*, 'Faith and Reason', 20 October 2001.
4. Masao Abe, 'There is no Common Denominator for World Religions: The Positive Meaning of this Negative Statement', *Buddhism and Interfaith Dialogue*. Part one of a two-volume sequel to *Zen and Western Thought*, edited by S Heine: Macmillan, 1995.
5. David Tracy, *On Naming the Present: Reflections on God, Hermeneutics, and Church*, New York, Orbis Books: SCM Press, 1994, p xii.
6. Richard King, 'Questioning the terms of the "dialogue" between faiths', *Dialogue and Difference: An International Conference*, University of London, School of Oriental and African Studies, September 2001.
7. Paulo Gonçalves, 'Religious "Worlds" and Their Alien Invaders: A

Deconstructive Perspective on the Representation of Religious Identity', in P Goodchild (ed) *Difference in Philosophy of Religion*, Aldershot: Ashgate (forthcoming).

8. Ibid
9. Op cit, Tracy: 1994, p 15
10. The former refers to the absolute power of the Sant (true)/guru person, in contrast with the more democratic Khalsa (pure ones) notion coupled with the notion of the True-Guru as being everywhere present and speaking.
11. See Richard King, *Orientalism and Religion: Postcolonial Theory, India and 'The Mystic East'*, London: Routledge, 1999, chs 2, 5, 7.
12. B Malinowski, *Argonauts of the Western Pacific*, New York: E P Dutton & Co, [1922] 1961, p 8.
13. From 1700s and beyond World War [11], 'Britain and France, and to a lesser extent Spain, Portugal, Germany, Russia, Italy, and Holland, dominated – ruled, occupied, exploited – nearly the entire world. By 1918, European powers had colonized 85 percent of the earth's surface' Tejaswini Niranjana, *Siting Translation: History, Post-structuralism, and the Colonial Context*, Berkeley: University of California Press, 1992, p 7.
14. Op cit, Tracy, 1994, p 131.
15. See Edward Said's *Orientalism: Western Conceptions of the Orient*, London: Penguin, 1991; Harjot Oberoi's *Construction of Religious Boundaries: Culture, Identity and Diversity in the Sikh Tradition*, Delhi: Oxford University Press, 1994.
16. However it must be stated that contemporary anthropology and ethnographic writing is now well aware of its own genealogy and orientations, and has moved beyond simple re-presentations of the other. See, for example, James Clifford and George Marcus (eds) *Writing Culture: the Poetics and Politics of Ethnography*, Berkeley, London: University of California Press, 1986; James Clifford, *The predicament of culture: twentieth-century ethnography, literature and art*, Cambridge, Mass, London: Harvard University Press, 1988; Arnold Krupat, *Ethnocriticism: ethnography, history, literature*, Berkeley, California, Oxford: University of California Press, 1992; Charlotte Aull Davies, *Reflexive ethnography: a guide to researching selves and others*, London: Routledge, 1999.
17. Karl-Heinz Kohl, 'Against Dialogue', *Paideuma* 44, 1998, pp 51-58, p 53.
18. Ibid, p 52.
19. Leonard Swidler, *Theoria to Praxis: How Jews, Christians, and Muslims can together move from Theory to Praxis*: Peeters, 1998. See ch 2

'Dialogue Decalogue', ch 14 'A Universal Declaration of a Global Ethic'. Note the slippage from three Semitic religions to the universal and so inclusive of all religions. The commandments in brief: 1. Purpose of dialogue is to learn (change, grow and understand reality and *then* act accordingly), 2. It must be a two-sided project, 3. Requires complete honesty and sincerity, 4. Must not compare ideals with your partner's practice, 5. Each participant must define himself, 6. Have no 'hard and fast' assumptions about points of disagreement, 7. Dialogue can take place only among equals, 8. Dialogue requires mutual trust, 9. Each participant must be at least minimally self-critical, 10. Each participant eventually must attempt to experience the partner's religion or ideology 'from within', pp 24-29. This naïve form of 'colonial anthropology' with its adoption of early phenomenological ideas as understood within the field of Religious Studies (empathy, bracketing etc), have been heavily criticised from a wide body of literature.

20. Op cit, Tracy: 1994, p 20.
21. Mikhail Bakhtin, *Problems of Dostoevsky's Poetics*, ed Caryl Emerson and Michael Hoquist, Austin: University of Texas Press, 1984, p 287.
22. Tejaswini Niranjana, *Siting Translation: History, Post-structuralism, and the Colonial Context*, Berkeley: University of California Press, 1992, p 3.
23. Ibid, p 2.
24. 'Translation is formally and pragmatically implicit in *every* act of communication ... be it in the widest semiotic sense or in more specifically verbal exchanges. To understand is to decipher. To hear significance is to translate. G Steiner, *After Babel: Aspects of language and translation*, Oxford: Oxford University Press, [1975] 1992, 2nd edn p xii.
25. Op cit, Bakhtin: 1984, p 110.
26. Edmond Jabès, *The Book of Margins*, trans Rosemary Waldrop, Chicago: University of Chicago Press, 1993, p 174.
27. Maurice Merleau-Ponty, *The Visible and the Invisible*, ed Claude Lefort, trans Alphonso Lingis, Evanston: Northwestern University Press, 1968, p 179.
28. Edmond Jabès, *The Book of Dialogue*, trans Rosemary Waldrop, Middletown, Connecticut: Wesleyan University Press, [1984] 1987, p 27.

Can our Religious Roots Provide a Route to a Harmonious World? – a Bahá`í View

Pamela Sutton

Shrinking world

Scientists talk about an expanding universe but we also say the world is shrinking! This is neither a new revelation nor a physical fact, merely an observation about how most people perceive the world today. A century ago, 40-mile journey times were the equivalent to those of 4,000 miles today. Visual communication was limited to face-to-face contact and communication by letter with the other side of the world took weeks, but now in our global society using modern day technology these things take only seconds.

A natural corollary of our shrinking world is an increased awareness of people who are different from our accustomed norm. Our neighbours and work colleagues no longer hail solely from the same village but can be from anywhere in the world. These new neighbours bring with them numerous differences encompassing a variety of aspects, including food, culture, traditions and religion. It may be argued that religion is the facet that affects people's minds and hearts the most deeply, as it concerns the bedrock of their very being. Consequently when people encounter others holding strong beliefs in a different faith from their own they may perceive this as a challenge, if not a threat, to their own beliefs. Heated arguments may emerge and animosity grow or, conversely, an invisible barrier of non-communication may develop.

Multi-faith concepts

Thus multi-faith concepts have necessarily emerged from our global neighbourhood, as a means of overcoming such problems in our pluralist society. The old adage about 'fear of the unknown' is particularly relevant when applied to faith. Fortunately, familiarity and understanding are powerful aids to cementing friendships at both individual and community level. The multi-faith ideal is, therefore, based essentially on raising awareness and on improving communications and understanding between people of many and varied faiths in the hope that they will become more tolerant and will co-exist peacefully. The term *multi-faith* may conjure up an image of a single eclectic faith, an amalgam of many, but this is an inappropriate and wrong image. Central to the multi-faith ideal is the acceptance of people's worth, the worth of their faith, and their right to follow and worship according to their religious tradition. Clearly there is no mixture here, no fusing of faith, but rather the opportunity for different faiths to be valued and respected alongside each other and for understanding, friendship and harmony to be fostered.

The Bahá`í Faith fully supports both the multi-faith ideal of tolerance towards other religious faiths, and the acceptance of their worth, and also encourages dialogue between faiths to promote understanding and co-operation.

However, the Bahá`í Faith extends this acceptance of worth further, to the actual acceptance of each of the major faiths as being valid and part of an overall theistic plan. A little history is needed to explain the Bahá`í viewpoint.

Bahá`í history

In 1844, a central figure within the Bahá`í Faith emerged in Persia. He adopted the title the Báb, meaning the gate. He declared himself to be the Twelfth Imám expected by the Shí`ih Muslims. Although a Manifestation (see later) in his own right, the Báb said his main mission was to foretell the imminent advent of another Prophet who was to be the 'Promised One of All Ages'. Hence the Báb`s title, the Gate, signifies an opening towards a new era. He prepared the way for this Promised One in a similar manner to John the Baptist preparing the way for Jesus. During the short 19 years of the Báb's dispensation thousands of His followers, Bábis, were persecuted for their beliefs and 20,000 died as martyrs.

The founder of the Bahá`í Faith, Bahá`u`lláh, born in 1817 of a noble Persian family, heard of the Báb, recognised His position and became one of these many followers. Bahá`u`lláh from an early age displayed an aura of wisdom and knowledge.

> He had an extraordinary power of attraction, which was felt by all. People always crowded round Him. Ministers and people of the Court would surround Him, and the children were also devoted to Him. [1]

Despite his noble birth Bahá`u`lláh declined an influential position within the government, preferring to work among the poor. He was imprisoned because of His Bábi beliefs, suffering abusive treatment including the bastinado. During his imprisonment in Tihrán in 1853 Bahá`u`lláh received a revelation that He was the Promised One foretold by the Báb and He adopted the title Bahá`u`lláh, meaning 'the Glory of God'.

Bahá`u`lláh was later banished from Persia, moving to Baghdad. There, in 1863, He declared His mission to his followers within the Bábi community who then became known as Bahá`ís. Bahá`u`lláh declared Himself to be the latest in a series of special prophets sent by God to guide mankind in its development on earth. His ever-increasing popularity was perceived by the established divines as a threat, so Bahá`u`lláh was exiled to Constantinople, then Adrianople and, finally, the prison-city of 'Akká, north of Haifa in what is now Israel. Bahá`u`lláh spent the remainder of his life there. He was imprisoned for a total of 40 years. Fortunately, during this time he was able to write many books, prayers and tablets (letters) which place the Bahá`í Faith in the enviable position of having in its possession the actual written word of its founder.

Bahá`í beliefs

So how do Bahá`ís regard their faith in relation to other faiths and in particular the multi-faith concept? This is determined by the status given to each religion and its founder. Bahá`ís call the prophets of God, 'Manifestations', as they manifest the perfect attributes of God, even though they are, themselves, innately human. The status of a Manifestation may be likened to regarding the sun in a mirror; it reflects all the qualities of the sun, but obviously is not the sun. Similarly a Manifestation reflects God's attributes, but is not God himself.

> These sanctified mirrors, ... From Him proceed their knowledge and power; ... these Primal mirrors which reflect the light of unfading glory, are but expressions of Him Who is the Invisible of the Invisibles. [2]

Bahá`ís regard the founders of all the major religions as Manifestations sent by the same God. Each was correct for their particular time and place in history and the essence of their teachings was consistent because of their identical source.

> He hath manifested unto men the Day Stars of His divine guidance, the Symbols of His divine unity, and hath ordained the knowledge of these sanctified Beings to be identical with the knowledge of His own Self. Whoso recognizeth them hath recognized God. ... Whoso turneth away from them, hath turned away from God, and whoso disbelieveth in them, hath disbelieved in God. [3]

Thus, Bahá`ís believe in one God, unknowable in essence. They also believe in one religion, the religion of God. This religion may manifest itself differently at various times and places in history. If religion is regarded as being composed of two parts, a fundamental similarity may be acknowledged between different faiths. The first part in all religions is concerned with man's relationship with God and his fellow beings, addressing the virtues of loving one another, honesty, selflessness, truthfulness, compassion and justice. Each Manifestation encourages his followers to adopt these same essential verities, which hence are evident in the lives of the followers of all the major faiths.

The second part concerns the social laws and regulations of a religion; each Manifestation may adapt these according to the different circumstances and needs of their particular time. These may appertain to how, where or when the followers may pray; or they may relate to dietary habits more suitable for their particular environment; or they may encompass dress codes again appropriate for their particular circumstances. Hence this part of each religion is recognisably different.

> There can be no doubt whatever that the peoples of the world, of whatever race or religion, derive their inspiration from one heavenly Source, and are the subjects of one God. The differences between the ordinances under which they abide should be attributed to the varying requirements and exigencies of the age in which they were revealed. [4]

Unfortunately, these social teachings and traditions are the outward, visible display of many religions today and to the uninformed they emphasise the differences between religions, creating barriers to understanding. The essential verities different religions have in common are not so clearly visible. This is where multi-faith activities are invaluable in enabling people to see beyond the mere visual diversity and become aware of the underlying similarities.

Bahá`ís regard each Manifestation as one and the same, showing the same perfect attributes of God to which mankind should aspire. Therefore to make any distinction between any of the faiths or their Manifestations is fallacious in the extreme.

> Beware, O believers in the Unity of God, lest ye be tempted to make any distinction between any of the Manifestations of His Cause, or to discriminate against the signs that have accompanied and proclaimed their Revelation. ... the works and acts of each and every one of these Manifestations of God, nay whatever pertaineth unto them, and whatsoever they may manifest in the future, are all ordained by God, and are a reflection of His Will and Purpose. Whoso maketh the slightest possible difference between their persons, their words, their messages, their acts and manners, hath indeed disbelieved in God, hath repudiated His signs, and betrayed the Cause of His Messengers. [5]

This is a fundamental of the Bahá`í Faith.

> Know thou assuredly that the essence of all the Prophets of God is one and the same. … There is no distinction whatsoever among the Bearers of My Message. … To prefer one in honour to another, to exalt certain ones above the rest, is in no wise to be permitted. [6]

Bahá`u`lláh refers to this succession of Manifestations as progressive revelation by God, describing how God imparts knowledge and guidance to mankind via his Manifestations in ordered and developing stages, according to our state of readiness and receptivity.

> … each Manifestation of God hath a distinct individuality, a definitely prescribed mission, a predestined revelation, and specially designated limitations. Each one of them is known by a different name, is characterised by a special attribute, fulfils a definite mission, and is entrusted with particular Revelation … [7]

For example, to talk about a world faith 2,000 years ago was neither appropriate nor practical. Knowledge of the globe was in its infancy and worldwide communications non-existent. Today, however, with modern communications and travel, talk of a world faith is quite feasible.

Thus Bahá`ís regard all the major religions highly and make no distinction in status between them as they all emanate from the same source, God.

> This is the changeless Faith of God, eternal in the past, eternal in the future. [8]

Interestingly, some modern theologians, Hick [9] for example, may agree with the commonality of each religion's source, a transcendent reality, but prefer to regard each religion not as a separate entity, but as different human responses to this same reality. In other words the source of their interpretation is human, with theistic traditions incorporating the concept of a deity and non-theistic traditions concentrating on the concept of the absolute.

In contrast the Bahá`ís believe that each religion is God-inspired rather than merely a response by man seeking to interpret the ultimate reality. However as Momen [10] points out, Hick's model is very similar to the relativism of the Bahá`í faith in which many differences in describing God or the Absolute can be attributed to differing cultural influences and varying modes of cognition. Momen also emphasises the Bahá`í belief that religion is evolving, not at a metaphysical, ethical or theological level, but at a social level. The Bahá`í concept of progressive revelation focuses on God as being the source of all revelations:

> different stages in the eternal history and constant evolution of one religion, Divine and indivisible [11]

The latest of these stages, the Bahá`í Faith, is an independent religion with its own Manifestation, Bahá`u`lláh, and its own sacred writings, calendar and holy days. Although Bahá`u`lláh emerged from a Muslim environment his revelation and subsequent teachings are completely independent, much the same as Christianity emerged as an independent religion despite the Jewish background of Jesus.

> I was but a man like others, asleep upon My couch, when lo, the breezes of the All-Glorious were wafted over Me, and taught Me the knowledge of all that hath been. This thing is not from Me, but from One Who is Almighty and All Knowing. And He bade Me lift up My voice between earth and heaven, ... His all-compelling summons hath reached Me, and caused Me to speak His praise amidst all people. I was indeed as one dead when His behest was uttered. The hand of the will of thy Lord, the Compassionate, the Merciful, transformed Me. [12]

Thus, Bahá`u`lláh does not claim any exclusivity regarding His position, nor interestingly does he claim to be the final Manifestation, rather He gives due notice that after at least a thousand years another prophet will appear. Therefore, to Bahá`ís, the multi-faith concept of people from different faiths meeting, communicating and increasing their understanding and appreciation of each other's faiths is a small but very necessary step for mankind towards facilitating harmony throughout the world. Whether this ultimately develops into the wholehearted acceptance of different faiths as part of God's preordained plan rests mainly on whether or not the vision is viewed through the eyes of a Bahá`í.

Diversity within unity

The Bahá`í Faith is greatly concerned with world unity, the promulgation of world peace, and building a society focused on the oneness of mankind.

> It is not for him to pride himself who loveth his own country, but rather for him who loveth the whole world. The earth is but one country and mankind its citizens. [13]

Bahá`ís believe this unity can only be brought about when mankind is united in its heart not just in the mind. In other words, people may talk logically about world peace, but when they feel their innermost values are being challenged, when something close to their emotions such as their religion, is challenged then resentment, often followed by retaliation, may ensue with disastrous results.

History is filled with examples that illustrate this sorry state. Devoted followers of most of the major faiths have bravely and determinedly defended their beliefs from what they perceived to be a threat from the followers of another faith. The differences rather than the similarities have always been uppermost in the warring minds. Past conflicts in the name of religion have often involved secular issues such as land or power. The true devotees of religion, for whom loving God and one's neighbour was the priority, have been quietly pushed aside in the mêlée of heated hostilities. Abdu`l-Baha, the son of Bahá`u`lláh, said in Paris:

> Religion should unite all hearts and cause wars and disputes to vanish from the face of the earth, give birth to spirituality, and bring life and light to each heart. If religion becomes a cause of dislike, hatred and division, it were better to be without it, and to withdraw from such a religion would be a truly religious act. For it is clear that the purpose of a remedy is to cure, but if the remedy should only aggravate the complaint it had better be left alone. Any religion which is not a cause of love and unity is no religion. All the holy prophets were as doctors to the soul; they gave prescriptions for the healing of mankind; thus any remedy that causes disease does not come from the great and supreme Physician. [14]

This illustrates where the followers of a faith should concentrate their attention. If people of all faiths focused on the innermost essence of faith, the essential verities, love, rather than ritual or doctrine, then history would not be so full of holy wars. Even today our present world manifests examples of suspicion and hostility fed by how humanity has interpreted religion, not by the fundamentals of the faiths as initiated by their founders. In giving guidance on how to live together, the original Manifestations of the main religions all preached the familiar 'do unto others as you would have them do unto you' philosophy.

Unfortunately instances of 'religious' strife have an additional effect beyond the immediate consequences. They are perceived by the non-religious as an intrinsic characteristic of religion and an indictment against it. The intolerance, narrowness of vision and prejudice of those engaged in religious strife are taken as indicative of the essence of faith, serving to repel people from religion altogether.

Bahá`ís believe Bahá`u`lláh was sent by God to refresh religious belief, to guide mankind and create again a spirit of understanding and love. Only when people are united in their hearts, through their religion, loving the same God and caring for each other as brothers and sisters under the auspices of a common faith, will the peoples of the earth come close to acting as peaceful parts of a united whole. This central theme of unity and the oneness of mankind is repeated again and again in Bahá`u`lláh's writings, leading to the ultimate aim of world peace.

> Ye are the fruits of one tree, and the leaves of one branch. Deal ye one with another with the utmost love and harmony, with friendliness and fellowship. [15]

Indeed Bahá`u`lláh not only encouraged His followers to mix freely with other faiths but positively enjoined them to do so.

> It is incumbent upon all the peoples of the world to reconcile their differences, and, with perfect unity and peace, abide beneath the shadow of the Tree of His care and loving-kindness. [16]

This concept of world unity and peace may seem utopian but it must surely be acknowledged that modern-day communication and travel facilities make the possibility of world unity more realistic than in previous ages. In addition, an ideal of perfection may be thought preferable to no ideal at all; and if such an ideal is God-inspired then it becomes a possibility in the humble mind of mankind.

However, it must be stressed that world unity does not mean uniformity; globalisation must not be allowed to reduce mankind to a monoculture. While recognising the equality of people the Bahá`í Faith emphasises the need to celebrate their ethnic and cultural diversity. Likening the human race to a garden, it would surely be dull if all the flowers it contained were always of the same kind; similarly the multiplicity of people's religious and cultural roots is a source of variety to be appreciated.

> The diversity in the human family should be the cause of love and harmony, as it is in music where many different notes blend together in the making of a perfect chord. If you meet those of a different race and colour from yourself, do not mistrust them and withdraw yourself into your shell of conventionality, but rather be glad and show them kindness. [17]

When someone becomes a Bahá`í, they do not negate nor devalue their previous faith. They merely move on to the next chapter in a book of progressive revelations from God, still psychologically maintaining their roots and belief in the previous chapters. Thus on a practical level, new Bahá`ís will recite the obligatory prayers, observe Bahá`í holy days and attend feasts; in addition they will find that they can continue to enjoy most of the celebrations from their original tradition if they so wish. No rigid form or programme is laid down for worship on Bahá`í holy days, only a general framework that can incorporate the flavours and influences from previous traditions. Each community may have its own particular biases and preferences. This can be seen within the present Bahá`í community where Native Americans may incorporate traditional dances in their feast, whereas a West Indian Bahá`í community may utilise more singing and Bahá`ís in the east, hailing from a Buddhist background, may adopt a quiet, meditative atmosphere. The peoples the world over are so very different, it is only natural for individuals to gravitate towards an ambience attractive to their customs and nature. Being united in one religion does not dictate uniformity in how people express their love for God and humanity. Thus as Smith explains:

> The Christian could continue to read the gospels and be inspired by the words and example of Jesus. The Muslim could continue to learn and recite the Qur`an in Arabic. The Jews could continue to take part in those festivals that celebrate their history and tradition as long as they adapted those that referred to the promise of the Messiah to show that the promise is now fulfilled. The Buddhist could continue with the forms of meditation that their traditions have developed and which they find of benefit. The Hindu could continue to offer puja to the gods and receive prashad. [18]

This is not eclecticism but a method which safeguards the autonomy and initiative of individuals and allows them personal freedom of worship within a framework of unity as revealed by Bahá`u`lláh.

Moving towards Unity

Over the years Bahá`ís have applied Bahá`u`lláh`s teachings practically, either instigating processes or supporting various international bodies which have encapsulated the multi-faith principle. In 1893 the World Parliament of Religions in Chicago heard the first mention of the Bahá`í Faith in the West, when its 'sentiments so noble, so Christ-like' (Henry H. Jessup [19]) were shared with the audience. Links with this organisation are maintained today. In 1959 the Bahá`í National Assembly of the United States inaugurated World Peace Day, which in 1985 developed into the United Nations International Day of Peace. Indeed the Bahá`ís actively support the United Nations, recognising it is as a valuable international body working against injustice. The Bahá`ís are one of the non-governmental organisations consulted by the UN on many current topics including women's issues, world peace and the environment.

At local, national and international level, Bahá`ís are supporting organisations concerned with new global ethics. This is an exciting paradigm where the multi-faith concept has developed beyond mere tolerance, dialogue and understanding between faiths, important as they are. It has grown into active co-operation between representatives of different faiths leading to the convergence of ideas and values focused on significant social, economic and moral issues. People of different faiths are engaged in discussion and are producing consensus documents which set out a common position on many issues such as the promotion of sustainable development, promoting justice as a prerequisite for peace, the eradication of poverty, the need for women's equality and the full implementation of human rights.

The Bahá`í Faith fully endorses these new advances within the multi-faith principle because the convergence of ideas and values from different faiths has the capacity to revitalise the role of religion in world affairs, returning it to its rightful place as a guiding instrument for human progress. Global harmony is regarded as spiritually imperative in a world in which the Creator moves His creation towards higher levels of concord and understanding.

Bibliography

1. `Abdu`l-Baha in Esslemont (1952), *Baha`u`llah and the New Era*, Wilmette, Illinois: Bahá`í Publishing Trust, p 28.
2. Bahá`u`lláh (1949), *Gleanings from the Writings of Bahá`u`lláh*, trans Shoghi Effendi, 2nd ed, Birmingham: Bahá`í Publishing Trust, p 47.
3. Ibid p 49
4. Ibid p 216
5. Ibid p 59
6. Ibid p 78
7. Ibid p 52
8. Ibid p 136
9. J Hick, *An Interpretation of Religion*, Basingstoke: Macmillan Press, 1989.
10. M Momen, *The Phenomenon of Religion*, Oxford: One World, 1999, p 73.
11. Shoghi Effendi (1938), *The World Order of Bahá`u`lláh*, Wilmette, Illinois: Bahá`í Publishing Trust, p 114.
12. Bahá`u`lláh, *The Proclamation of Bahá`u`lláh to Nasiri`d-Din Shah*, Haifa: Universal House of Justice, 1967, p 57.

13. Bahá`u`lláh (1949), *Gleanings from the Writings of Bahá`u`lláh,* trans Shoghi Effendi, 2nd ed Birmingham: Bahá`í Publishing Trust, p 249.
14. `Abdu`l-Baha (1961), *Paris Talks*, 10th ed, London: Bahá`í Publishing Trust p 130.
15. Bahá`u`lláh (1949), *Gleanings from the Writings of Bahá`u`lláh,* trans Shoghi Effendi, 2nd ed, Birmingham: Bahá`í Publishing Trust, p 287.
16. Ibid p 6
17. `Abdu`l-Baha (1961), *Paris Talks*, 10th ed: Bahá`í Publishing Trust, p 53.
18. Peter Smith, 'The Bahá`í Faith and Religious Diversity', in *The Bahá`í Studies Review*, vol 1. 1: Association for Bahá`í Studies, 1991.
19. Henry H Jessup, in Shoghi Effendi (1958) *God Passes By*, Wilmette, Illinois: Bahá`í Publishing Trust, p 256.

'Not a Load of Moonshine' – A Pagan Contribution to a Multi-Faith Britain

Steven Rumelhart

It is a sunny afternoon. A car speeds its way through an Alpine valley and passes a panoramic viewing point where several artists sit at their easels painting. We look briefly at the paintings and see a watercolour, an oil painting, a Cubist and an Impressionist rendering: several different ways of viewing the same mountain, a range of styles and colours depicting the same scene. This imagery is not my own, but comes from a television advertisement for a popular small car a few years ago and serves as an analogy when considering a Pagan contribution to the concept of multi-faith debate. It is an idea I shall be returning to when considering how dialogue can promote tolerance and understanding between differing religions.

> The rise and growth of Paganism in this country is inextricably linked to the change in the religious landscape of Britain in the latter half of the 20th century. A brief overview of the last 50 years helps us to understand how we have arrived at the situation we find ourselves in today.

The post-war years saw a huge influx of people and ideas arriving from all over the world, adding to this island's already rich and divergent religious life. For perhaps the first time, many people were brought into contact with faiths and religions other than monotheism. The Education Act of 1944 contained provisions for Religious Instruction (RI), but over the coming decades, as Britain became more ethnically and religiously diverse, it soon became apparent that RI (later Religious Education or RE) provided inadequate teaching about the full range of other people's religious beliefs and practices. As a consequence, the promotion, understanding and tolerance of other religions were seriously impeded for many years.

Meanwhile, almost unnoticed by the majority of people, the little-known and rarely enforced mediaeval Witchcraft and Vagrancy Act was repealed in 1951. If Britain was soon to witness the arrival of new and 'exotic' religions from abroad, it would have been all too easy to overlook a phenomenon about to mushroom and grow on its own doorstep, namely 'the only religion England has ever given the world; that of modern pagan witchcraft' (Hutton 1999).

Over the next decade the fact that witchcraft was no longer considered a crime allowed many practitioners of what they called 'the craft' to become more open about their beliefs and practices and to write about them. Self-imposed 'witch ethics' (and an understandable desire for secrecy – this was still the 1950s) meant little more than that history and a 'read between the lines' approach was adopted, giving no more than hints as to what witches really did and believed. This in turn gave rise to much sensationalist tabloid 'reporting' where the misleading and lurid tone was defamatory and very harmful to what were, in the main, harmless individuals following Wicca, a religion they believed to be a continuation of a centuries-old tradition revering nature and harming none.

Society, however, was changing too. The 1960s witnessed an explosion of free-thinking and what were seen then as radical new ideas. People were experimenting with alternative concepts and different ways of living in both the religious and secular worlds, often with much overlapping of the two. Valiente (1985) believed:

> A great alteration in human attitudes and behaviour took place in the decade of the sixties, much to the alarm of conventionally minded people. It has been called the sexual revolution, the swinging sixties, the advent of the permissive society and so on; though a lot of it is simply the frankness of Uranus bringing out into the open what was there anyway, but discreetly hidden behind a polite cloak of humbug.

This mutation in our society was heralded by a remarkable astronomical event. On the 5th February 1962 no less than seven heavenly bodies were foregathered in the sign of Aquarius. These were the Sun and Moon, and all five of the planets visible to the naked eye, namely Saturn, Jupiter, Mars, Venus and Mercury. Astrologers the world over discussed this phenomenon, and it was generally agreed that it marked some sort of turning point in mundane affairs, especially as it occurred in the sign of the New Age.

Doreen Valiente, who followed Gerald Gardner (1884-1964) as one of the pioneers of modern Wicca, opens the introduction to her book, *Witchcraft for Tomorrow*, with the words 'This book is written as a contribution to the Aquarian Age'.

Astrologers, mystics, occultists and some sections of contemporary paganism alike agree that the motion of the Earth, planets and stars can be mapped and plotted, giving us astrological ages. As any astrologer will tell you, the constellation Aquarius (the Water-Carrier) has two ruling planets, Saturn and Uranus. Saturn symbolises all that endures and all that is rooted in the past, along with ancient wisdom. Uranus however stands for all that is new, revolutionary, strange and even bizarre.

If the 60s and early 70s saw a growth in prosperity, an increase in leisure time and increasing experimentation with styles and exotic cultures amongst the young, all this came to a halt with the advent of the 80s and what have come to be known as 'the Thatcher years'. It was this decade of almost Orwellian 'greed is good' politics that paradoxically brought the 'New Age' movement and, as a consequence of this, contemporary Paganism in its present form to the attention of the public at large.

If certain sections of society found the yuppies and their high-spending, high-profile consumerism with grossly over-inflated salaries and egos to match offensive, it was not long before the 'have nots' sought solace in the spiritual. Had a hard day aspiring to a high-flying career in the City? Why not relax in a soothing aromatherapy bath? Not enough noughts on your bank balance? Why not light a candle and repeat your wealth-generating affirmations? 'Discover the wealth and health secrets of the ancients on this special audio cassette – yours for only ...' Selling people a spirituality of sorts became big business.

What has become known as the New Age movement of the last decade did help to put many alternative ideas and spiritualities into mainstream public awareness. Herb lore, candle burning, Bach Flower Remedies, which were once mostly of interest to Pagans and a few alternative health practitioners, can now be found in most high streets and shopping centres the country over, and innumerable publications of varying quality can be found in many local bookshops promising everything from being able to talk to an angel to being able to turn your ex-partner into a frog! If Paganism's first task was to tackle much of the stigma and misunderstanding to which it was subject, it now finds itself having to defend its credibility.

Contemporary paganism is often confused with the New Age movement and does share many superficial attributes with it, but this quotation attributed to Margot Alder succinctly illustrates one of the key differences between the two worldviews:

> There is a funny saying in the pagan movement: The difference between pagan and 'New Age' is one decimal point.

In other words, a two-day workshop on meditation with a New Age practitioner might cost £300, while the same course by a Pagan might cost £30.

Pagans may feel some amusement towards the New Age movement but they acknowledge that it has made acceptable much that was previously the province of Paganism alone. Consequently, Pagan belief and practice is no longer regarded as strange, frightening or deviant. Can a ceremony at full moon for global peace and world healing by a Pagan be any odder than a City analyst consulting a Feng Shui expert about her interior decorating?

The New Age and the New Aquarian Age Valiente writes about are synonymous but not mutually exclusive. The 90s saw Paganism consolidating its position with organisations such as the Pagan Federation working with the media to counter adverse reporting and to inform schools, parents and teachers accurately about the practices and beliefs of those calling themselves Pagan. A series of academic conferences was held at universities across the country to consider aspects of Paganism and a number of subsequent high-quality publications became available to academics and the general public alike, clearly setting out the origins of contemporary Paganism.

A recent article in *The Sunday Times* reported, 'In England in 1990 there were 5,000 practising pagans; now, according to a study by Newcastle University, there are 100,000 – outnumbering Britain's 80,000 Buddhists.' An extensive study by Hutton (1999) found figures to suggest 'the existence of between 90,000 and 120,000 non-initiated Pagans in Britain.' If these figures are correct, this means there are 10,000 people per year choosing to express their religious feelings and sentiments through Paganism, making this one of the fastest-growing religions in Britain today. Having seen how the rise and growth of a native spirituality, born of an age of change and in tune with and responding to the spirit of the times we live in, has come to a position of prominence within the religious landscape of Britain today, we will now consider some of the beliefs of contemporary Paganism and consider what it can bring to the multi-faith debate.

Paganism today does not claim to possess any 'ultimate truths'. It is a religion rooted in the earth we live on and share, and it recognises that there is more than one way of honouring and worshipping the gods and goddesses of all peoples. Pagan theology is a cluster of theologies, since Paganism is nothing if not a polytheistic religion where many different threads interweave, complement and sometimes contradict each other.

Druid Emma Restall Orr writes, 'It is a pantheism. It guises itself as a polytheism yet declares many gods to be aspects of the one light or the divine mother/father. The monotheism of Mother is also prevalent.' Something for everyone, it would appear, and it could be argued there are nearly as many Pagan theologies as there are Pagans. Ultimately, arguments over who is right or wrong are futile and so it remains that 'many of these [beliefs] are not formulated and not debated by the Pagan community, but form a taken-for-granted background to religious practice' as Prudence Jones (1996) writes when commenting on Pagan approaches and assumptions about the relationship between Pagans and the divine. This is not through ignorance on the part of the Pagan practitioner since most Pagans own many books on their particular area of interest and research it diligently, be it Wicca, folklore, ecology or gardening. It is just that theology really is not that important to Pagans. The closest that contemporary Paganism comes to having a specific belief is recognising that divinity may manifest in female form, and although many Pagans feel that the divine transcends gender, the worship of the goddess is integral to many Pagan paths.

Just as the four images of a mountain that the four artists produced may be equally valid, so a Druid with a particular affinity with the Celtic or Anglo-Saxon pantheons would not dismiss a Witch directing prayers to Diana or Hecate as being misguided. Such gods are all aspects of the divine in Paganism's eyes. Just as the mountain is always the mountain, there are many ways of seeing it. Each of us feels drawn to expressing our religion in our own way towards the gods or goddesses of our choice and all ways are equally valid. This is a matter of personal choice and one would not dream of telling another practitioner that her way was wrong. If I do not profess to be right, how can I say she is wrong?

Paganism has no set texts or gurus, no liturgy or dogma. This is not to say that Paganism has no ideas and beliefs of its own, but rather that:

> Paganism is not centred around the worship of deities. Pagans may have invented theology – and some are deeply concerned with feminist theology – but a concern with correct and fervent belief is not common in Pagan discourse. Seasonal festivals are more indicative and formative for Paganism than the names or nature of particular Goddesses and Gods.
>
> Graham Harvey 1997

Many Pagans feel that they have an affinity with certain deities and honour them in their own way. There is no 'Pagan orthodoxy' and there are no priests or priestesses to prescribe how to worship. Where a priestess or priest is involved it is usually in the role of a facilitator or to act as a focus for group ritual but certainly not to say what is to be believed. Put simply, there is no right or wrong way in contemporary Paganism about how to express oneself with regard to the divine: all are free to be their own priestess or priest. It is more the case of the *integrity* the practitioner brings to the sacred space with Hutton (1999) commenting: 'It is the only religion to make a religious virtue out of self-expression'.

Many Pagans today see themselves as spiritual rather than religious and many are even atheists yet '... this Pagan Atheism in no way diminishes the celebration of those things in Paganism which seem to be more central than worship and theology, the celebration of nature, the land and the festivals' (Graham Harvey 1997). Pagans come to a sacred space and take part in seasonal observances or ritual with their own ideas about the divine, and it is here in sacred space that differences enrich rather than detract from the experience. Like a good stew or curry, all the different flavours make up a tasty whole. Indeed, it has been the experience of the author to have attended seasonal celebrations where Wiccans, Druids, heathen and representatives from an indigenous Polynesian religion all contributed to the opening and closing of the sacred circle at the Summer Solstice in Avebury in 1996 and, despite the best efforts of other faiths, few have achieved such success in incorporating so many divergent beliefs in religiously pluralistic worship. Similar gatherings have seen Native Americans, Quakers, Buddhists and European Shamans all participate.

It is this eclecticism that makes Paganism today such a rich and exotic mix. Despite some strands of the craft claiming to go back to antiquity, by and large contemporary Paganism is a religion no older than about 70 years. As a religion in its relative infancy, Paganism has been able to draw upon and borrow from much of modern thinking and thus avoid many of the pitfalls of the older, well-established traditions, such as the dividing of religion into two different aspects, the 'mystical and individual on the one hand, and the organisational on the other' (Maslow 1974). It is ironic that what makes contemporary Paganism so attractive to many and is considered one of its greatest strengths can also be seen as its biggest flaw. Paganism's relative infancy means that it has no central focus or organisational hierarchy and certainly no one set of ethics to which all practitioners adhere. The focus is instead mainly on the individual's personal choices. There is no dogma either, and while this frees Paganism from becoming stagnant, personal experiences and introspection may detract from a collective and shared sense of direction and purpose. Maslow believes, however, that 'the profoundly and authentically religious person integrates these trends easily and automatically'. He goes on to say:

> What this all adds up to is this: small 'r' religion is quite compatible, at a higher level of personal development, with rationality, with science, with social passion. Not only this, but it can, in principle, quite easily integrate the healthy animal, material and selfish with the naturalistically transcendent, spiritual and axiological.

Paganism has 'grown up' in an age that saw vast and sweeping changes to the religious landscape of Britain. The influx of differing religions has enabled contemporary Paganism to draw upon the polytheistic approach of the Hindus, the mysticism of the Sufis, the meditational practices of the Buddhists as well as humanistic and psychotherapeutic thinking. As Jones remarks, 'The tolerance and flexibility of a polytheistic outlook, allowing many ways, many goddesses and gods, many philosophical schools in keen dispute with one another, is that of a religion that is suitable for our multicultural, postmodernist age' (Jones in Harvey and Hardman 1996). Let us now look at Pagan contributions to multi/interfaith dialogue before considering what all faiths can gain from that dialogue.

Initially, pagan involvement in interfaith dialogue consisted of little more than attempting to end defamation and discrimination. Once basic misunderstandings were cleared up – Pagans do not sacrifice babies or worship the devil – a rudimentary acceptance of Paganism developed. For the most part, the only sacrifices Pagans make are those of time and energy organising covens, groves or moots and denying infanticide and devil-worship. Still, it was the case that many felt uncomfortable with these eccentric individuals, and attempts were made to find some common ground and areas of mutual interest. It was with some relief that it was discovered that Paganism is very concerned about environmental issues. This led to the well-meaning but somewhat patronising inclusion of Pagans sitting in on interfaith debates as little more than the 'green conscience' of such groups, focusing entirely on such secular issues and overlooking Paganism's potential to enrich dialogue between religions.

'Dialogue is an encounter that aims to improve the understanding and respect between two or more parties. It does not require agreement but it does require honesty.' Harvey goes on to say that 'Dialogue is easier for Pagans than for many religionists because they are not obsessed by proving the truthfulness or universal applicability of their tradition' (Harvey, p 216). As we have seen, Paganism asserts no absolute truths and it is this lack of dogma that leaves it free to engage in honest and open dialogue with other faiths as it has no hidden agenda or point to prove; does not feel the need to try and convert others, and nor does it seek to prove that its way is the right way.

If we see interfaith dialogue as not so much point scoring but as a way to facilitate mutual understanding and an appreciation of one anothers' beliefs and traditions, we could liken the exercise to that of listening collectively to an orchestra. One individual could say how much they appreciated the string section while another may prefer the brass. Yet another may draw attention to the percussion section and how much they liked that. While each may have her personal preference for certain sections of the orchestra, by listening together and drawing attention to her particular preferences her overall appreciation for the piece of music is increased. It is not of vital importance to me whether the person I am listening with agrees with me that the string section is the best part of the music, just that we hear it within the whole and appreciate it within that.

By listening, and in turn being listened to, we are better able to understand not only the beliefs of people of other faiths, but our own faith too. As Max Müller said, 'The person who knows only one religion does not know any religion'. So it is for a Pagan reading the Qur'an, the Dhammapada, the Ramayana, or standing watching the sunrise from Stonehenge at the Summer Solstice. Each of these may increase an aspect of understanding and increase faith.

Mark Graham, the Pagan Federation's current Interfaith Officer, believes 'Pagans generally welcome diversity and colour and are usually freer to express themselves in a multi-faith/multicultural environment where a range of belief systems exist. For this reason I think most Pagans would welcome the development of a multi-faith Britain where their religion was afforded the same respect as anyone else's.' It is hoped that after reading this chapter not only will the reader have a better understanding of contemporary Paganism and what it can offer but also see why its inclusion here is not only timely but imperative.

Britain is fast becoming a multi-ethnic and multicultural society and sooner or later everyone will come into contact with people, ideas, cultures and religions that they may well find 'odd', challenging or even frightening. Prejudices, misconceptions and misunderstandings do exist and it is one of the challenges facing all of us to try and eradicate them. These sentiments are not mere platitudes. Events recently in Burnley and Oldham and elsewhere have clearly shown how religious zealotry can be used to 'justify' the most horrific of acts, and history is riddled with religious persecution. There is cause for optimism though. The Education Reform Act of 1996 has now made it compulsory for children to be taught about the teachings and practice of all the principal religions in Britain and this, it is hoped, will lead to future generations having an increased understanding and tolerance of faiths other than their own. It may soon become a criminal offence to discriminate in the United Kingdom on the grounds of religious persuasion and some sections of the popular media have produced excellent programmes and articles on the religious beliefs and customs of all the world's faiths. Whether we choose to believe in the idea of the Aquarian Age or not, it is notable that Aquarius, astrologically speaking, stands for communication and a universal brotherhood. Perhaps Aquarius is the ideal sign for the 'Information Age' and the much-heralded 'Global Village' ?

Bibliography

Harvey, G, *Listening People, Speaking Earth*, London: Thorsons, 1997.
Hutton, R, *The Triumph of the Moon*, Oxford: Oxford University Press, 1999.

Jones, P, in G Harvey and C Hardman, *Paganism Today*, London: Thorsons, 1996.

Maslow, A H, *Religions, Values and Peak Experiences,* London: Penguin/Arkana, 1974.

Valiente, D, *Witchcraft for Tomorrow*, London: Hale, 1985.

A Diverse Universe of Values – A Greek (un-)Orthodox Perspective

Manos Hatzimovos

There is a day for everyone of us in our existence when we become conscious and aware that we just are. We did not ask or choose to be here, we are just here. Some of us come into this world with the full use and potency of our senses, others do not. Some of us are born into affluence and plenty, others into poverty and want. We are all born with varieties of skin colour, different genders and ethnicities. We all experience our lives in different locations of the world and in different class locations, within matrices of differing worldviews. For all our variety and difference we share one thing in common: we all need to express ourselves to the people around us and to a 'greater beyond'.

Born in Rhodes, a small isle south east of Greece, and being indoctrinated in the Christian Orthodox tradition, I too felt the need to question the reasons for my existence and learn to divine a purpose. In a nation where religion holds a highly symbolic, yet passive role in everyday affairs, little room is left for sincere introspection and critical evaluation of beliefs and values. Historically, the Christian religion has been the arbiter of the high aspirations of the Greek people for their liberation after 600 years' occupation under the Ottoman Empire. Therefore, the open questioning of such traditional fundamentals of the Greek State and culture have generally not been perceived as entirely edifying.

When I migrated to multicultural Britain, a kaleidoscopic spectacle, I found that it had grown out of a rich amalgam of civilisations and its impression on my senses was as fierce as its impact was on the formation of the world map. Through the religious tolerance that has gradually become part of the national ethos since the 1770s, Britain is currently host to communities of Bahais, Buddhists, Christians. Hindus, Jains, Jews, Muslims, Sikhs and Zoroastrians who make a substantial contribution to the British cultural status quo. An atmosphere of interdependence is evident where in many places communities have successfully negotiated appropriate local arrangements such as providing religiously acceptable food in hospitals, making adequate provision for funeral requirements and creating prayer rooms in institutions used by all faiths.

Overall, the contemporary British scene could be referred to as the 'spiritual supermarket' where customers are free to pick and mix their own proffered religious brands – or not to buy at all. Personally, I found myself pandering to my strongest consumerist urges without considering the possible repercussions of a 'spiritual overdose'. Admittedly, neither did the majority of my fellow students. Bombarded with teachings on yoga, reiki, tai chi, acupressure, homeopathy, transcendental meditation and everything else, an individual might well experience what Carl Jung termed 'enantiodromia', the pursuit of one direction until one ultimately ends up at the opposite.

From the interplay of opposing feelings of engagement with living, and an awareness of having gained a new-found value-orientation (feeling that certain things matter), I found myself in the role of International Students' officer, on the Executive Committee of Derby Students' Union, promoting cultural integration and opposing ideological discrimination.

I experienced the challenges of integration without assimilation in the academic and wider community. The question has been raised more than once in the past: what is essential to one's religion and what can and should be adapted to the British context? Perhaps authentic integration is the key, which calls for adjustment from society at large to become more genuinely inclusive.

Albert Einstein once speculated that science without religion is lame, while religion without science is blind. In the same way, one could assume that culture without diversity is sterile and diversity without the realisation of one's culture is elusive and potentially dangerous. In the shadow of recent events of global terror and dissolution of order, the world needs to understand that religious beliefs once defined as morally wrong can further promote disaster through backwardness and division. In order to avoid religious prejudice and secularised isolation of faith communities, religion needs to be understood in terms of geography and history and not through absolute, dogmatic claims of 'truth-exclusiveness'.

The 'supermarket' analogy can jeopardise the respect for each individual's integrity. It fails to recognise what potential the great faiths have for co-operation rather than just competition. Hence, a realisation needs to be made that it is just possible to trace shared values across communities and faiths. Commitment to justice, care for the natural world, valuing of family life, recognition that the common good for all can only be found through seeking higher, spiritual ends – these and other common themes resonate across all faiths.

The element of communion that one experiences through spiritual worship can be characterised as essentially 'erotic'. The term 'erotic' functions for me in several ways. Mostly, it serves to describe the power which comes from sharing deeply any pursuit with another person. The sharing of joy, whether physical, emotional, psychic or intellectual, forms a bridge between the sharers. That can be the basis for understanding much of what is not shared between them, and lessens the threat of their perceived difference. In Sanskrit, the word 'satsang', which translates into English as 'meeting', means a 'godly gathering'. In the English language the word 'common' is linked through the word 'communicate' to 'communion'. To exist in a state of communion is to be aware of the nature of existence. This is where ecology and social justice come together, with the knowledge that life is held in common. Whether we know it or not, we exist because we exchange, because we move the gift. The knowledge of this is as crucial to the condition of the soul as its practice is to the body.

Today, however, there seems to be no place given in the world economy, governed by the profit motive, for the cultivation and nourishment of the spiritual life. Worship, contemplation and silence have no value in this system because none of these activities is governed by the motivation of profit. People who attend to their spiritual life are seen in this as non-productive or even as underdeveloped.

This is precisely what I have savoured the most in an institution that enfolds religious dialogue on the scale that the University of Derby does. The place and time where students, revolutionary citizens of the new era of conscious self-awareness, the privileged ones who escape the short-sighted mechanistic rush for a common world, can proclaim their secular independence and declare their responsibility to cultivate and nourish the openness of nature and humanity, and respectfully to see the multiplicity and creativity of cultural creations in the tapestry we call life. To develop attitudes of outrage and responsibility in the face of injustice and oppression, and to strive for harmony, peace, and justice through a world of love, compassion, community and interdependence within the tradition of democratic principles. Furthermore, these creatures of the millennium recognise the need to contemplate the awe and mystery of the universe as it reflects the eminence of life in harmony.

It is with great conviction that I affirm the transformative impact a multi-faith Britain had on my idiosyncrasy. I felt open to rethink how I saw others, the world and myself. I encountered culture and myself anew. Amidst a culture where inter-religious, inter-cultural, inter-ideological, inter-disciplinary, inter-personal dialogues abounded in all directions, my former identity was both challenged and reformulated. I felt my former unilateral way of thinking an impossible place to return to. Now, I have the foresight to realise that it is not a state of independence that I seek to obtain, but rather an inter-dependence within my spiritual and physical environment. It is the realisation that the self is not the highest authority; it is the ability of the self to commune with others and the diverse spiritual forces that surround us that is the more authentic state of being.

Is Multi-Faith Religious Education Multi-Faith Enough?

Philip Knight

According to the American philosopher, Richard Rorty (1989), the modern individual faces two responsibilities: one to herself, the other to ensuring that in exercising this first responsibility she does not tread on anyone else's toes. This second responsibility calls for qualities such as empathy, tolerance, understanding and care in order to create a real sense of human solidarity, which is sensitive to the pain and humiliation that our actions might cause others. This alone justifies the multi-faith approach to religious education (or religious studies if you prefer that term) currently being taught in Britain's schools. I suggest, however, that the first responsibility is, perhaps, less well served by current multi-faith RE which does not give enough room for students to consider that their own passions, experiences and commitments are religious in nature.

Most state schools in England and Wales follow a locally-agreed syllabus of religious education. National guidelines set out in two model syllabuses by the School Curriculum and Assessment Authority in 1994 suggest that young people leaving school should have had the opportunity to 'acquire and develop knowledge and understanding of Christianity and the other principal religions represented in Great Britain' (SCAA 1994 p 4). One, not untypical, locally-agreed syllabus based on these guidelines aims to have students learn to 'appreciate the diversity of religious belief and practice and the rights of others to hold beliefs different from their own' (Kent County Council 2000 p 11). This means that RE departments in schools throughout the country have, in recent years, increasingly become mini centres of multi-faith learning.

Students are required to engage in a systematic study of up to six world religions (Christianity, Judaism, Islam, Hinduism, Buddhism and Sikhism) and relate the teachings of these religions to shared human experiences. Each religion (three in any key stage) is to be studied as an integral whole and 50% of the teaching time is to be devoted to Christianity. Students are also required to learn *from* as well as *about* the religions they study, developing in the process a range of skills appropriate to understanding the beliefs of others. These skills include: the ability both to investigate, interpret, evaluate, express and reflect upon the beliefs, practices, texts and symbols of the religions they have studied and also to empathise with what it is like to be a follower of these religions. When learning *about* a religion students are required to show that they understand that religion's facts by identifying, describing and explaining its important features, for example knowing when, how and why Muslims perform Hajj or Jews celebrate Pesach. In learning *from* a religion students are encouraged to reflect on the meaning which aspects of that religion might have for their own lives, for example assessing the relevance to their own way of life of the great teachers and teachings of a religion or what the Sikh rite of Amrit chhakna or the Christian rite of confirmation might say to the commitments that young people increasingly have to make as they grow and develop.

This is an obvious improvement on both the confessional approach which reduced all RE to a study of Christianity, and the study of religious phenomena, which tended to reduce religious differences to a common set of human practices. The new syllabus allows students to develop a picture of the major religions which they are likely to encounter in the world outside of school and gives teachers a clear set of criteria against which to assess a student's progress. Although specialist RE teachers often have to implement this multi-faith approach with the assistance of teachers for whom RE is not their main subject, an improvement in the standards of RE in schools is becoming evident.

However, there is a pressing problem. Among a majority of students there is still a feeling, captured statistically by Leslie Francis (1996 pp 223-246), that religious belief is *for others* and that the subject should have no place on the school curriculum. It seems that while many students relate what they learn in RE to the experiences of their everyday life they find little of direct relevance to their growing self-understanding. Students who do not consider themselves to be represented by any of the major faiths they study may mistakenly come to understand themselves as being non-religious. If you work with the assumption, as I do, that everyone is religious in some way or, in the words of the Christian educationalist, Jeff Astley, that 'everyone does theology and everyone has a theology, however thin, incoherent, unsystematic and irrational' (Astley and Francis 1996 p 70), you accept that the religious dimension of experience must be understood as extending beyond what is captured within the major religious faiths. Thus the sense of irrelevance that many students attribute to RE may arise because RE is still not multi-faith enough.

In Key Stage Four (age 14-16), the Kent Agreed Syllabus offers for study two core units, 'Aspects of Christianity' and 'Aspects of [one of the other five] Living Religions'. It also suggests two further units of study from a list of 12. This list includes the Baha'i faith and Oriental religions. However, recognising a broader religious dimension to experience beyond the six major faiths that students are required to study does not mean adding more religions to the list of what is to be studied in school. Nor does it mean following unit seven in the Kent syllabus, 'Atheism, Agnosticism and the Humanist Tradition'. Such a unit certainly merits greater emphasis because it allows students to look beyond the particular religions they have studied for alternative answers to life's questions, but, isolated in the syllabus, it seems to suggest that if none of the religions studied fits students' self-understanding the only alternative they have is to assume they are non-religious.

A more completely multi-faith RE syllabus could avoid this problem by recognising a broader definition of the religious aspects of life than is found within the major religions alone. These broader, more indeterminate dimensions of religious experience have, perhaps, been best articulated by the American pragmatist and educationalist, John Dewey. In his book, *A Common Faith*, Dewey distinguishes between the multitude of religions and the religious quality of experience they embody. He writes:

> It is widely supposed that a person who does not accept any religion is thereby shown to be a non-religious person. Yet it is conceivable that the present depression in religion is closely connected with the fact that religions now prevent, because of their weight of historic encumbrances, the religious quality of experience from coming to consciousness and finding the expression that is appropriate to present conditions, intellectual and moral. ... I believe that many persons are so repelled from what exists as a religion by its intellectual and moral implications, that they are not even aware of attitudes in themselves that if they come to fruition would be genuinely religious.
>
> Dewey 1934 p 9

For Dewey, the religious dimension of experience does not depend on a specific set of doctrines, texts or practices nor need it be organised into a particular cultural system. Rather, he writes, 'It denotes attitudes that may be taken toward every object and every proposed end or ideal' (ibid p 10). The religious dimension is identified by the *effect* it has on a person's life. It is related to significant moments in a person's life, to times when their whole being is turned around or opened up 'bringing about a better, deeper and enduring adjustment in life' (ibid p 14). Dewey associates this broader understanding of life's natural religiousness with the imagining of ideal goals; the union between these goals and their active realisation; the joys of a free participatory democratic spirit; open scientific inquiry and the recognition that the individual is dependent on both the community in which she lives and the wider world.

Identifying what is religious in students' experience, Dewey believed, means taking into account their own powers, interests, impulses and initiatives. For contemporary religious educators this could mean recognising their students' involvement in such indeterminate dimensions of religious experience as devotion to football, pop or fashion culture; their reflections on the (religious) significance of *Star Wars* and *Star Trek*; and practices of witchcraft, new age fads and even Presleytarianism (Elvis cults). What distinguishes these dimensions of religious experience from the more discrete determinate faiths is that students are not yet tempted to deny that religion is primarily something humans do. These dimensions are examples of what John D Caputo, following Jacques Derrida, calls 'religion without religion'.

For Caputo, as human beings we cannot avoid being religious in the same way that we cannot avoid being political. For him, it is in the exchange between the determinate and indeterminate faiths that genuine religious creativity and an openness to transcendence (expressed as an openness to 'the other that is to come') take place. In this creative religious space, non-knowing is the religious inspiration. In my experience as an RE teacher, when students talk honestly about religion it usually finds them in this open space. This space emerges out of the interplay between the various 'religious' passions which students currently happen to be 'into' and the determinate faiths they study. As Caputo puts it:

> It would never be for me a question of choosing between a determinate religious faith and this faith without faith that does not know what it believes or who we are, but rather of inhabiting the distance between them and of learning how to let each unhinge and disturb – and by disturbing, deepen – the other.
>
> Caputo 2001 p 36

What I am advocating, then, is a broader understanding of multi-faith education in which the involvement of students in various indeterminate faiths is recognised and reflected throughout religious education. As Dewey makes clear, this broader dimension to religious experience would resist the type of systematic articulation which would be required for it to be included as a discrete unit within an RE syllabus. However, its inclusion as a theme within existing units is certainly possible and would allow students to acknowledge the religious dimension of whatever it is they are 'into', perhaps thereby deepening their own appreciation of the major faiths they study. A broader multi-faith syllabus could include among its aims the desire to allow students the space to recognise their own passions, questions and commitments as being religious in character. It might suggest that the delight taken in a poem, a picture, a piece of music, a sporting achievement, a sunset or even another person can be religious in character. It might ask students to discuss what does and does not count as religious using, for example, 'Homer the Heretic', an episode from the television series, *The Simpsons,* as stimulus. It might suggest that teachers should occasionally emphasise the non-knowing that may arise from a comparison between equally plausible but contrary religious positions. It might ask students to keep a diary and to make a note of the significant ideas, events, people, beliefs, and attitudes that seem to be guiding their life as they move through the school term or year. It might suggest that students compare football or Presleytarianism with Ninian Smart's seven dimensions of religion. [1] It could suggest that teachers read Caputo's analysis of the religious meaning of *Star Wars* (Caputo 2001 pp 67-90) in order to ask students to make a comparison with one of the major faiths they study.

This broader multi-faith approach would help to redress the situation in which the majority of students encounter religious belief as outsiders. In an essentially secular education system, accepting Dewey's challenge to emancipate what is religious in experience from its exclusive association with the particular creeds and practices of the major religions should, in my view, be the future task of religious educators. This may even lead to the questioning of the distinction between the religious and the secular that has tended to confine the religions to specific, often non-controversial, areas of cultural life. This broader multi-faith approach needs far more development than I can give here [2] but something very like it is necessary if young people are to recognise the connections between the faiths they study and the faith-commitments and practices they engage with everyday of their lives.

One post-modern writer who recognises these connections is Gianni Vattimo. He notes that:

> A secularised culture is not a culture that has simply left behind the religious contents of its tradition; it is one that continues to live them as

traces, as models that are hidden and disfigured but nonetheless profoundly present.

Vattimo 1985 p 34

For Vattimo, the growth in various indeterminate religious faiths is part of a wider cultural shift toward pluralism, relativism and nihilism which has to be embraced as the continuation in 'weakened' form of past metaphysical religious systems of belief that are, nevertheless, still very much a part of our own cultural inheritance. For example, he argues that it is difficult to understand contemporary secular pluralistic culture without also understanding the Judeo-Christian mythology about a self-expending kenotic God, the God who expends and empties himself for others. He writes:

> ... secularisation is the way in which kenosis, having begun with the incarnation of Christ, but even before that with the covenant between God and 'his' people, continues to realise itself more and more clearly by furthering the education of mankind concerning the overcoming of originary violence essential to the sacred and to social life itself.

Vattimo 1999 p 48

This 'originary violence' he understands as the imposition on society of a monoculture guaranteed by a belief in a single, supreme metaphysical being. Overcoming this violence has turned out to be the vocation of western secular thought. As Vattimo would see it, six-religion multi-faith RE not only requires the inclusion of ever more human expressions of the religious dimension to life but actually actively promotes these other dimensions. Learning *about* and *from* the major world faiths promotes a non-violent religious pluralism and a secular tolerance that goes hand-in-hand with a greater self-critical recognition that religions are a revisable historical human creation. They are resources to be mined for future religious growth rather than present possessions to be protected and kept safe for eternity. Here, multi-faith learning turns syncretistic; a pick-and-mix in which students draw upon the discrete determinate religions they have studied to confirm, supplement, or even replace their own religious outlook. Carried to its logical conclusion such a process would rightly question the extent to which the major world religions are themselves properly conceived as discrete determinate entities. Indeed, many religious people today match their religious life to their needs by drawing from a wide variety of religious sources, taking little heed of traditional lines of demarcation. As the religious pragmatist, Sheila Greeve Davaney, puts it:

> Both conceptually and functionally, persons and communities all over the world construct ways of living in the world that are less concerned with purity of lineage and more with how varied traditions that influence them can be resources in the face of the ongoing and changing challenges of life.
>
> Davaney 2000 p 174

Dewey's point, with which Davaney is sympathetic, is that many of these resources will include a wide range of beliefs, commitments, rituals and experiences which the practitioners of the more explicit determinate faiths would not normally consider religious. The broader multi-faith understanding of religious education which I have been attempting to articulate here might lead to the type of religious culture that Richard Rorty has called 'secular polytheism'. This is a culture that has accepted Dewey's understanding of religion. It celebrates with William James the variety of religious experience, seeing with him the determinate faiths as 'secondary accretions' on experiences that renew themselves in the events of our everyday lives. It is a culture that Nietzsche described as 'permitted to behold a *plurality of norms*: [with] one god ... not considered a denial of another god, nor blasphemy against him' (1974 ed) p 191.

Rorty writes:

> To be a polytheist in this sense you do not have to believe that there are nonhuman persons with powers to intervene in human affairs. All you need do is to abandon the idea that we should try to find a way of making everything hang together, which will tell all human beings what to do with their lives, and tell all of them the same thing.
>
> Rorty 1998 pp 23-24

While current trends in religious education are moving in this direction it remains possible that the old confessional and phenomenological approaches still ride on the back of a limited six-religion multi-faith RE. A broader base to multi-faith learning is thus called for which continues to study the major world religions represented in Britain but which also allows students to recognise their own passions and commitments as religious in character even though they may have little connection with religion's traditional forms. This, as Dewey readily admits, may sound harsh in the ears of followers of the determinate religions but, like him, I believe it is necessary to wrest away from their hold the monopoly they too often claim over the religious dimension of experience. It is this, rather than their own expression of this dimension of experience, that, in Dewey's words, 'stands in the way of the realisation of distinctively religious values in natural experience. ... Just because the release of these values is so important.' He adds, 'their identification with the creeds and cults of religions must be dissolved.' (Dewey 1934 p 27-28.) Like Dewey, Caputo describes a religion as a human artefact but he immediately adds that it is structured so as to articulate the love of God. Caputo understands this love as an open and challenging question, 'What do I love when I love my God?' Is it God whom I love or is God the name I give to what I love? There is no answer. We have to live with and in the ambiguity and with the various diverse religious passions it creates. 'If God is anywhere,' he says, 'it is in the diversity.' (Caputo 2001 p 131.) Multi-faith religious education, however it is understood, could not find a better motto to adopt than this.

References

1. Ninian Smart sees no reason to doubt that his seven dimensions of religion can be made to fit what might be regarded as purely secular commitments. Ninian Smart, *The World's Religions*, Cambridge: Cambridge University Press, 1989, 2nd ed, pp 22-26.
2. See Philip Knight, John Dewey's 'Religion in Our Schools Ninety Years On', in *British Journal of Religious Education*, vol 20, 1998, pp 70-79.

Bibliography

Astley, Jeff, 'Theology for the Untheological?: Theology, Philosophy and the Classroom' in Jeff Astley and Leslie J Francis, *Christian Education and*

Religious Education: Connections and Contradictions, London: SPCK, 1996.

Caputo, John D, *On Religion*, London: Routledge, 2001.

Davaney, Sheila Greeve, *Pragmatic Historicism: A Theology For the Twenty-First Century*, Albany: State University of New York Press, 2000.

Dewey, John, *A Common Faith*, New Haven: Yale University Press, 1934.

Francis, Leslie J and Lewis, John M, 'Who Wants RE?: A Socio-psychological Profile of Adolescent Support for Religious Education' in Jeff Astley and Leslie J Francis, *Christian Education and Religious Education: Connections and Contradictions*, London: SPCK, 1996.

Kent County Council, *Responding to Religion: Engaging With Living Faiths*, Maidstone: KCC, 2000.

Nietzsche, Friedrich, *The Gay Science*, (E T Walter Kaufmann) New York: Vintage Books, 1882 (1974 ed).

Rorty, Richard, 'Pragmatism as Romantic Polytheism' in Morris Dickstein *The Revival of Pragmatism: New Essays on Social Thought, Law, and Culture*, Durham: Duke University Press, 1998.

Rorty, Richard, (1989) *Contingency, Irony and Solidarity*, Cambridge: Cambridge University Press, 1989.

Schools Curriculum and Assessment Authority, *Religious Education: Model Syllabuses Model 1: Living Faiths Today* London: SCAA, 1994.

Vattimo, Gianni, 'Myth and the fate of Secularisation' (E T Jon R Snyder) in *Res*, vol 9, 1984.

Vattimo, Gianni, *Belief*, (E T Luca D'Isanto and David Webb), Cambridge: Polity Press, 1999.

Faith for the Future – The Role of the Young in a Multi-Faith Britain

Benjamin E Kerr-Shaw

The experienced professionals of public house philosophy will tell you the knack is to keep your mouth open and your mind closed. However, on this occasion I let my guard slip and must admit to coming precariously close to spilling my Carling upon hearing my friend's latest theory. Young people, he claimed, do not need God. The sober, less-slurred, translation of his argument went something like: in our pleasant, genetically modified, ready-made, artificially intelligent age we simply no longer depend on some all-powerful, benevolent nanny to soothe our angst and suffering. Gerry Springer, Radiohead and the occasional spliff are usually sufficient to obscure the painful rays of reality that interrupt our mind-numbing, daily searches for the next essential item that will make our lives complete. For once, I endeavoured to give the matter a bit of thought before replying – the classic amateur error.

OK, so in the midst of our hedonistic existence we may have lost touch with the bigger picture, I argued, but that does not mean young people are going to stop believing in God, they are just rejecting all the moral responsibility that goes with it. Apparently I had misunderstood my friend's proposal. It was not, he claimed, that we no longer believe in God, just that we have no use for the big fella anymore. I have slightly fuzzy memories of thinking this proposition was a touch more contentious then the first, and so would excuse an even longer period of reflection before responding. This moment never came, however, as the clock tolled 10 and I pointed out it was high time we departed for some other den of sin where the music was far too loud to communicate in anything but sweeping hand gestures and physical assault.

A hangover is rarely a catalyst to deep, meaningful thought, but the next day I strove to draw a moral from this episode. The fact is that I suspect that my friend is not the only disillusioned young person out there. Cynicism at such a tender age and in those who have so many hopes, dreams and disappointments before them is surely a little unhealthy. Still, it is an attitude that can be easily understood. In a multi-faith Britain the younger generation feels redundant. This is nothing new, but when pressure is being exerted on us to build a more inclusive society, the usually harmless, rebellious nature of the denim-clad masses may prove dangerous. Let us consider then how we should change this trend and prepare ourselves, regardless of belief, for a world of many different faiths.

Why is it important to learn about faith? It is a question I keep asking myself, along with how am I going to pay off a mortgage with a theology degree. It speaks volumes that your average teenage Briton learns about religion in the classroom and not in a church. Teaching religion as an academic subject and not as a way of life in many ways undermines the very idea of faith. Nor is it easy for a child to learn about religion and science or history through the same medium, a Harry Potter-crazed 10-year-old should not be making subtle distinctions between knowledge and justified belief. However, an objective, scholarly method could well be one route to a harmonious multi-faith society. The classroom approach to religion equips us to become sceptical towards dogma and encourages us to search for the reasons behind someone's faith. When we can understand why a person holds a particular belief we are able to see them as an individual and not merely as a clone.

Teaching religion in schools can easily avoid the obvious difficulties of religious education within a faith community. For example, it is hard for a Sunday school not to merge all other faiths into one category of 'other religions', thus fuelling early 'us and them' attitudes. Perhaps, most importantly, schools are the ideal environment in which an objective yet involved understanding of religion can be learned.

The issue of whether multi-faith education is multi-faith enough is explored in the previous chapter. On this matter we must tread with caution. What use is it for us to be able to name the five pillars of Islam when we cannot grasp that each Muslim has their own personal thoughts, opinions and moral code? Are we working towards a more inclusive society when we can recognise a man in a turban as a Sikh, but not as an individual? Knowing about religion without knowing about people is dangerous. Even more dangerous is the trend of categorisation within religions. Being given a label and classed in a particular sect of a particular branch of a particular faith only encourages prejudice, especially amongst academics. It is not sufficient to teach that faith comes in many different flavours; the child must learn that there are as many flavours as there are believers.

It is perhaps appropriate here to cite my own religious education as evidence that a one-faith perspective can restrict a child searching for the answers to the 'Big Questions' to a very limited philosophical inventory. I cannot quite recall my theological ideology as a seven-year-old. I have blurred memories of it involving pilgrimage to the spinney at the back of the estate, weekly homage to the A-Team and the occasional sacrificial offering of a daddy-long-legs or two. For me, and I suspect most other Thundercats fans, 'church' was the act of being dragged away from the children's programmes on a Sunday morning and being shipped off to learn that Santa used to be called Jesus Christ and that he could make wine out of five loaves and two fishes, or something like that.

A growing religious awareness must be one of the more bizarre parts of growing up. I remember arguing on my front lawn with my next-door neighbour after a particularly messy encounter with some innocent creature of nature about the implausibility of an omnipotent, benevolent creator from which we should adopt a workable ethical code of loving stuff and being nice to bugs. My side of the informed discussion was not going too well until I posed what I thought would be the death blow to her holy ranting:

'So who made God then?'

'God did,' came her reply. Darn it, bamboozled by a six-year-old redhead. Luckily I had one last ace up my grubby sleeve. By sending a large clot of mud in her general direction I thus proved the non-existence of an all-powerful being worthy of worship, who could have stepped in with a thunderbolt; being sent to my room without tea does not count as divine retribution in my book.

My most vivid recollection of growing up in multi-faith Britain was my first encounter with another religion. The lasting impression I got from visiting a temple with my mum was how similar the ways of religious practice are and, crucially, how self-evident it was that we were worshipping the same entity. Yet even with my basic (mis)understanding of the Bible I was simply unable to progress from this idea to a concept that there really was nothing to distinguish 'them' as being any different from 'us'. I was unable to see the individual. I was caught within a belief system that had imposed a sense of groupism upon me. Not by brainwashing or incitement to racism, but merely by providing a safe, internally coherent environment that I had never had cause to question. It was not until I was sat down, flicking pencils and scribbling on desks in a classroom that I began to see the differences in religion as cultural and not idealistic divides.

How do we enthuse the PlayStation generation to take an interest in multi-faith relations? Simple, just make the A-Level chemistry and biology syllabuses harder. Well, it worked for me anyway. Up until six weeks into my A-Level courses I had never given thought, not even at the height of my incense-burning phase, to returning to the RE lessons that had been compulsory for the last nine years. However, delusions of becoming a doctor were fading rapidly behind a barrage of negatively charged ions and unsaturated fat molecules. The sciences had to go. I had not seen eye-to-eye with the languages department since declaring English as the only lingo one needs to get by in the world. I still have the scars (and the herb rack) from my last encounter with the technology subjects and quite frankly art is an area best left to those with a more mature understanding of the human form. So it was I took a long, hard look at the options tick sheet before me: drama or religious studies. So, it had come to this. In a way, the decision was made for me from my previous experiences in the sphere of amateur dramatics – I look daft in tights, so that was that.

I never quite got my mates' jokes about sharpening my blue pencil crayon and practising drawing arms, as most of the gods that I would soon be colouring in had more hands then eyes. Nevertheless, although I would not realise it for some weeks, shyly shuffling into that female-filled room and announcing my intention to drop science and take up religious studies was the best decision I have ever made. I discovered that, unlike science and maths, religious studies is very much a two-way learning experience. It is hard to hold a personal viewpoint in the realm of equations, nor can you be argumentative in the face of the periodic table. Perhaps more than any subject, religious studies is about learning how to think, not what to think.

A religious education should not be founded on dogma and ancient scriptures, nor should it be based on a purely factual knowledge of history and statistics. When taught properly a religious education must be about people, their personal beliefs and their way of life. I was fortunate enough to be taught within an award-winning religious studies department that not only showed me the real importance of faiths but got me through my exams as well. The most important aspect of the course for me was being able to express an opinion without having to support it by quoting a prophet or scripture. To speak and write from one's own experience and judgment as opposed to recounting what you have been taught to say is truly liberating. For our children's sake this must be the emphasis for the future. Is it surprising that my generation see RE as 'colouring in the gods'? Their only experience of the subject comes from compulsory lessons aimed at acceptance, but this ultimately falls short of teaching that there is a person behind the believer. Freedom and responsibility can only come when we are allowed to think for ourselves.

A multi-faith society will not be born out of a careful examination of any scriptures. It will not be found in an enthusiastic academic's rewriting of the human psyche. No government legislation can alter our opinions. Tolerance, compassion and empathy within the British people can only be rooted in the hearts and minds of each citizen.

Education is a key factor in working toward this inclusive state, but there is another, which in practice has proved just as effective.

Apathy is currently the strongest force against religious tension. What is the first and greatest barrier any fundamentalist must overcome before converting a person to their cause? They must convince that person their cause is worth missing *EastEnders* for. Apathy has never thrown rocks at temples, apathy does not beat up taxi drivers and apathy strongly refrains from flying planes into buildings. The reason we are rightly fearful of apathy and fight against it in our schools, parliaments and places of worship is those qualities it breeds: ignorance, selfishness and a narrowed world view. By understanding the reasons behind this apparent indifference of the young we may find the path toward a multi-faith society.

If Christianity were still practised in the dank, echoing catacombs of Roman-occupied Palestine, or Buddhist meditation was taken in short breaks between fleeing the marauding Chinese armies in Tibet, then there would be no difficulty in persuading youngsters that religion is hip. Give an impressionable teenager a Kalashnikov with the instruction to fight for his beliefs and you have his soul. Asking him to sell jam for the church roof fund will not have quite the same impact. My point is that religion used to be, and still is elsewhere, a dynamic battleground of values, an opportunity to escape the tedium of daily life and even to kill people on principle. In my experience church is perceived to be a dull hobby, practised only by those who are not hung-over on a Sunday morning. So here lies the crisis point of multi-faith relations: how do we enthuse youngsters to value a belief-system and yet imbue them with a respect for the beliefs of others? Surely no two different belief-systems can both be true, therefore someone must be wrong, and so if you *know* your beliefs to be true – and this must be a predicate of any genuine *belief* – it must follow that you have a duty towards your tragically misinformed friends to lead them back from the dark side.

My naturally cynical generation can see straight past the smiling handshakes of religious leaders to the fact that each believer *knows* the other to be deluded. How can we promote religious acceptance in this atmosphere? Again, we find we must escape the institutionalisation of the religions and look to the individual. Many young people reject religion, but not necessarily the idea of a god or 'Ultimate Reality'.

I fear this is the point where I am meant to reassure the reader about how rosy the future of multi-faith relations is – that the next generation will heed the errors of their parents so that we can create a path to a genuinely inclusive society. I should apologise in advance. The greatest difficulty in creating a youth-orientated multi-faith society is that no one is exactly sure what it is we want out of the exercise. Presumably the government is looking for a diplomatic understanding between the faiths, in real terms a balance between burning temples and churches and an amalgamation of the faiths; yet any morally conscious organisation is a threat to the economy. As for the religious groups, it is hard to say if there is an aim at all. Certainly, moves towards promoting dialogue and harmony seem to be advanced by dedicated individuals, with often only the grudging consent of their respective organisations. Furthermore, although I cannot doubt the motives of such forward-thinking people, it may be wondered whether there is any blueprint or intended destination for multi-faith ventures. Is it perhaps a little dangerous embarking on such an ambitious journey without being quite sure of where it is we want to go? Then again, I guess if Mr Columbus had stayed at home on the sofa we might well be struggling to survive without fast food and shopping malls.

The role of the young in these changing times is still hard to define. Only in education through living, and so allowing our children to see through the barriers of cultural divide, can we best prepare ourselves for what lies ahead. Will we ever see a day where religion ceases to become a badge, and people can celebrate each other's beliefs? What is the best way to secure this future? Can we transmit our multi-faith values to the rest of the world? The truth is, I do not know. Sometimes it is best not to have the answer. We can sometimes think more clearly during silence than during a sermon. A faith that does not claim to grasp the ultimate truth, but only reflects, examines, and appreciates the splendour of the diverse universe around us is perhaps the faith we must now choose. It is a faith in each other.

From Handcuffs to Hands Clasped – from Christianity to Buddhism

Philip Henry

The determined taunts experienced at the hands of an angry crowd seem a distant echo in the memory of a now committed Buddhist. They were however very real, in a world where a Buddhist worldview offers illusory interpretation as an answer to all forms of human experience. I am that Buddhist and those angry words were aimed at me.

As a former police officer (of 18 years) my transition from a Christian background influenced by a secular lifestyle and work ethic, may seem to many an unusual, if not bizarre shift of influence in one's life. A not unreasonable assumption, taking into account the bigotry, violence and general uncertainty of a 'copper's lot', particularly in times of increased crime levels and suppressed police numbers, as was the case for the majority of my service.

I joined the police as a cadet from school at 16, it was either that or agricultural college. The police came up with the first offer, and not being considered an academic I snapped it up. I left home for the first time to endure what any squaddie would refer to as square bashing. The relentless morning parades and marching tunes are rooted firmly in my memory alongside that early morning dip in the unheated outdoor pool and cross-country runs that a catholic might find akin to purgatory.

My indoctrination and ultimate education included methods of self-defence, exposure to CS gas, and a drill sergeant, the thought of whom scared the life out of you hours before he roared in your ear.

'This is good for you laddie, isn't it? Tell everyone how good it is for you!' he screamed.

If you knew what was good for you, you screamed back whatever it was he wanted to hear. There was no room for negotiation or thoughtful reflection in this world of master versus pupil. You were there to learn, and learn you would by whatever method the master imposed.

My childhood experiences included a regular Sunday family service in our local C of E church. A must at 10am each week until I was 11 or 12, when a deeper commitment was expected. Far be it from me to disappoint parents or parson, so I went along to communion lessons and was confirmed into that family, the Church, a community I never really understood. However, I was a part of it and remained within the family as choirboy and pathfinder youth member until my eventual confirmation as a fully-fledged officer of the law.

At 18½ I was old enough to assume that mantle and was sent away for basic training at a former RAF base in North Yorkshire. The story was a similar one to that of the lowly cadet, only now I was the lowly PC. The barrack room mentality continued apace, with the added pressure of learning the basics of criminal law – a daunting task for most participants, but necessary in order to perform one's duties adequately once unleashed on the unsuspecting public.

A friend of mine in basic training made no secret of the fact that he was a Christian. The 'stick' he suffered made me cringe inside, for fear anyone should realise I'd only recently hung up my cassock as second bass in the choir of St Mary's. For a couple of weeks I wrestled with my Christian conscience. Should I offer him support or was I in for much of the same relentless ribbing if I did? The pressure to succeed overwhelmed my guilt, and I resolved to keep my head down in a cowardly stance to get through this earthly hell and back to my force with as little fuss as possible. The centre of my universe was passing the nightmare that was the weekly law exam, this occupied nearly all my waking thoughts, and a conflict over faith seemed highly inappropriate at the time.

After much marching, spit and polish of boots and pressing of uniform, the final pass-out parade arrived. I had completed the 10 weeks of trauma, and was alive and well to tell the tale. The discipline of a two-year cadetship had stood me in good stead, now it was time at last to become a fully functioning public servant. I acknowledge in retrospect that my next two years as a probationary constable put paid to many of my thoughts of a creator God, and begged me to question my own sanity at times, as well as that of those around me.

The world as I had known it involved the church, sport, scout troop and adolescent encounters with the opposite sex. It was a far cry from the world I now inhabited. It seemed that I was at the centre of a continuum. The police on one side, with pressure from superior ranks demanding success and results; and a public that seemed intent on either removing you from office, or removing your head from your body by whatever violent means they deemed necessary.

My impressions, like many young officers of the 70s and 80s were that solace was only to be found among your rank and file colleagues. Here a bond existed that offered a survival package to cope with life's injustices. I believe the camaraderie was stronger than family ties for a number of my colleagues. It often resulted in an inward-looking service banding together to repel the constant flak that fed the criminal populations, hierarchical bosses and politicians alike.

It was during the first five years of service that my attitude towards God changed, and questions of doubt about his creation of such a hostile world were constantly in my mind. These were personal issues, not for discussion among the group. Christian values were never evident, as an agenda item, either in work or outside. The social circles of friends that developed were in the main from within the police and the insular nature of my existence was a common theme among most of my friends.

I have vivid recollections of the sight of my first corpse, and that of my first murder scene. Equally durable are memories of abused children, beaten mothers and psychotic individuals, disturbed and capable of inhumane thought and action. This then was not a world to be taken lightly. It may sound as though there was only the underbelly of society participating in it, strangely that was how it felt. It was easy to overlook the good and the great making up the majority of the populace, when contact with them was limited by the constant immersion in life on the edge.

As time passed I became immune, in varying degrees, to many things: to death, violence and its results, people in all forms of distress, verbal and physical abuse and the innate ability of human beings to ride roughshod over their fellow man in their effort to succeed, fuelled by greed, hatred and delusion. This is not to say that my attitude to humanity was tainted to the 'tarring of all, with the same proverbial brush'. What it did, in fact, was to suppress my own levels of anxiety and thereby allow the reduced adrenaline to act as a buffer to the otherwise knee-jerk emotions that these events were capable of provoking.

My mother questioned my values several times, on rare visits home. 'This job's making you hard, lighten up a little,' she'd say.

As far as I was concerned I was perfectly normal, doing well at work, with an active life at the gym, on the golf course and in the pub, what more could one strive for? The only serious hiccup seemed to have been my early marriage (at 19) to my childhood sweetheart, separation a year later, and subsequent divorce. Perhaps my parents saw this as evidence of a lifestyle that fundamentally changes one's personality. I saw it as things not working out and having got married too early due to parental pressures on both sides, and a fear of doing otherwise.

As a young detective, life progressed at an alarming rate, and various specialist departments allowed me to take in many more experiences and activities, to which others with similar service on the beat were not subject. With it came innumerable visits to the Crown Court where one learned another skill, that of survival through the power of words. The battlefield was across oak panels and wigs, against barristers whose sole ambition often appeared to be the art of reducing a witness to a gibbering wreck for the benefit of his client's liberty. Notwithstanding the responsibilities to their clients, the route they took was often more akin to the crimes they were defending, rather than the justice it was inspired to seek.

I met and married my second wife within the confines of the police service. Our children were raised in suburbia where a mix of good citizenship and Christian values were offered in a largely secular world. That was until that fateful winter night when an arrest, which was little more than routine, resulted in a scuffle and a fall that was to change my life in an instant. A snow-covered evening saw me at 'casualty' once more, not uncommon territory over the years, only this time I was on the treatment table. I came home in a collar with the usual words of wisdom for whiplash sufferers, prescribed by the tired house doctor. An uncomfortable night and increased agony saw my return to hospital in the morning. The rest is history: a spinal injury to my neck, three years of constant trips to hospitals and consultants, the constant wearing of collars in various forms and a pain threshold I didn't even know existed.

The net result of this unfortunate experience was removal from my job, a pension payout and bewilderment at where my life had suddenly disappeared to. My sole existence was now chair-bound with excruciating pain and fitful, sleepless nights, which were longer than the traumatised days. As a result I developed a sense of despair I had only seen in others. In the light of this trauma whole ways of life changed, not just for me but for those around me. My parents were called upon to help with the children and my wife who had been a hardworking housewife and mum was suddenly plunged into self-employment to sustain the family. As for me, I was as miserable, cantankerous and disparaging of the world as it was humanly possible to be.

Over the next four years I questioned my fate between analgesic highs, and when my wife determined to take me on a holiday, as much for my sanity as for her rest, I agreed. My first experience of the Far East was a frightening prospect. Would I cope with the flights, had I enough medication, what if …, what about … , if only …? The questions were relentless, and to add to my anxiety I had suffered strange heart rhythms inducing panic attacks, and therefore had become dependent on a beta-blocker. Despite my lack of confidence and clinical depression, the holiday went ahead.

Thailand has been described as 'East meets West' and by all accounts supports this description, however simplistic and superficial. The Thai way of life is framed in a way that supports the respect of kingship and state. With the greater intervention of Western economies and a strong Chinese influence since the Second World War it is not uncommon to find the Westerner grappling to understand the seemingly superficial Thai way of life. To stand humbly under, as opposed to characteristically above and looking down at Thailand, is alien to Western ideologies that acknowledge the so-called 'developing world' as inferior.

Thailand was my destination, a country and its people with whom I have developed a lasting relationship. What was it about Thailand that took me from the tourist to the Buddhist? – perhaps a little insight of my own. Thais have a consummate instinct for adapting to cultural situations in which relative status is the dominant factor. They tend to spend their lives more or less on the surface of things. We all do, to some extent. But the key lies in the Thai's ability to prove they can live daily without depth, while the rest of the world is busy proving that no matter how deeply they bury themselves in invigorating media hype they cannot do without surfaces.

On my return home I began to appreciate that the cultured Thai smile, attention to nuances of behaviour, receptiveness to outside influences, non-aggressive attitude and natural tact made the Thai a perfect world ambassador. The ability of a culture to invite approach yet defy explanation was enough to harness my curiosity to the spirituality of the culture. It is expressed in the state religion of Buddhism, which contains older Brahmanic and animistic forms in a strangely syncretistic style.

I purchased several books both in Thailand and the UK in an effort to understand something of this rich yet simplistic culture. The rose tinted glasses were on and romanticism without doubt was affecting my judgement. That was until I made contact with Phra Maha Laow Panyasiri, a Thai monk from the Wat Buddhapadipa Temple in Wimbledon, who had recently moved to Aston Buddha Vihara, Birmingham, to act as the spiritual guide to the Ambedkar Buddhist group that owned the temple.

My search for a Thai Buddhist connection in the UK had taken some time, but I was eventually advised by the Buddhist Society in

London of a Thai Temple in Handsworth Wood, Birmingham. On a visit I recall a dysfunctional conversation with a Thai monk Phra Peboon, who spoke little English to complement my almost non-existent Thai. He did however succeed in orientating me to the Aston Temple and explained that a Thai language class was about to begin there. My intention was to use the Thai language as a way of opening up its culture. Surely if I learned to speak Thai I could find the answers to some of my questions?

Phra Maha Laow was happy to enrol me on his language course and for several months I tried hard to learn the fundamentals. I am not, however, a natural language student, and still find the basics difficult. I was nonetheless drawn to the people and their culture. This was not, though, a Westerner in search of the mystic cave of the East climbing the canyon to Nirvana. Rather a realisation that the Thai's superficial surfaces gave them at least a halfway start to non-attachment and non-self that we in the West were still puzzling over.

The more I saw of the nature of the Thai community and their lives associated with the Temple, the more my determination grew to explore Buddhism at a deeper, more meaningful level. With that effort came the necessary and inevitable path to meditation, a cornerstone of all things Buddhist. So great was the 'desire' to learn that this very human attachment caused great confusion initially as it was explained in terms of an obstacle to my development. In Buddhism the way to self-realisation is to let go of the desire for and attachment to objects and relationships, which are seen as ultimately ephemeral and therefore impermanent.

The fundamental teachings of the Buddha were explained to me with great care and at this point I realised that the moral precepts of a Buddhist were essentially the same as those of the Christian, albeit without the acknowledgement of a creator God. Questions about this, the Buddha explained, were beyond human comprehension, therefore one's efforts were better generated in matters of the here and now. In this sense humans could have a personal effect upon their search for Nirvana (liberation). This made logical sense in a world where I found little comfort in a creator God.

The similarities between the Ten Commandments in Christianity and the moral precepts of a Buddhist were striking. I could see no logical reason why a Christian could not hold Buddhist values and vice versa. The moral and ethical code of Buddhism is also a reflection of the ethics of Sikhs and Muslims alike. The precepts, in their simplest form require one to refrain from killing, taking that which is not freely given, sexual misconduct, speaking falsely and avoiding intoxicants and drugs capable of clouding the mind.

Although Buddhists avoid the terms right and wrong and replace them with 'skilful' and 'unskilful' thoughts and actions, when analysed the similarities are clear. Many religions offer a moral ethic by which to live one's life, as does Buddhism. The desire of Christians to involve themselves in meditation is not new. Here the parallel with Buddhism is further evidence of its accessibility for other faiths. There have been several occasions in the last five years when Christians have visited the Buddha Vihara Temple in Birmingham and have participated in meditation. A Muslim man was a regular at the Thursday evening meditation classes. He said his Imam thought it unusual but did not object.

The five precepts of the Buddhist offer a positive counterpart in that they develop compassion and loving kindness to all living things, generosity, the cultivation of stillness, simplicity and contentment, truthful gentle purpose in speech and the development of mindfulness. These issues are seen in and by other faiths as positive and essential elements of human life. The development of the Bodhisattva (an enlightened being), whose vows in Buddhism are based on loving-kindness and compassion for all sentient beings, portrays a Christ-like quality in the desire to assist all beings before oneself. The close proximity of Buddhism to Christianity in this respect is overwhelming, accepting there is no notion of a creator God in Buddhism the moral fibre for daily life is appreciated and respected by other faith communities.

My personal association with 'Socially Engaged Buddhism' (a term requiring clarification) demonstrates to other faiths the Buddhist as a proactive member of society with an ability to act in support of the poor, war-torn and oppressed. This then is an area in Buddhism where the imperative of action is paramount, dispelling the 'other-worldly' stereotype that has troubled some Buddhists in the West.

The Buddha gave everyone the opportunity to understand the nature of being human. The self-realisation, which comes from insight-wisdom, developed through regular meditation practice and daily life practices of mindfulness. It is not a clever spin on an old tradition developed to succour romantic Westerners, but a realisation of the true nature of all phenomena. In so doing one eliminates craving (tanha) and hence Dukkha. Other faith groups would not deny that craving in life causes varying degrees of suffering. They may address the problem with different methods but acknowledge its causes in the same way, using different adjectives to describe them.

'Dukkha' is one of the singularly most important aspects of Buddhist teaching, and one that is continually misunderstood or misinterpreted. I use the 'pali' term 'Dukkha' as there really is no adequate English equivalent. It is often translated as suffering, or unsatisfactoriness, mental conflict, anguish, imperfection, frustration or disappointment. All these things can be Dukkha. There are three basic categories of Dukkha: firstly that caused by what we know as suffering in an ordinary everyday sense, both physically and mentally. The suffering caused by change, a more subtle type not normally recognised until a happy state changes and becomes less agreeable. Finally suffering caused by ignorance of one's own reality, and the true nature of the world. This leads to craving and clinging to things or situations, which are inherently impermanent. As Buddhists point out, unless we recognise the impermanent nature of all phenomena, including ourselves we can never be free of this kind of suffering.

The Buddha offered an explanation of Dukkha in the 'Four Noble Truths'.
1. There is Dukkha
2. Dukkha arises because of craving (fuelled by ego).
3. Dukkha ceases through the elimination of craving (tanha).
4. The 'Noble Eightfold Path' leads to the elimination of 'tanha' and hence to the cessation of Dukkha.

The subtle ways in which one should understand Dukkha does not mean that to practise Buddhism, and meditation in particular, one should become a depressed person, seeing misery in every aspect of our lives. When investigating Dukkha we can use our personal experiences in a dispassionate way to see it in its various forms. We should understand that the potential for Dukkha is inherent in all things and situations with which we come into contact. It is the reaction of our minds to these phenomena that determines whether that inherent Dukkha arises or not. Meditation will make this clear and allow you to begin to understand the truth of the second and successive statements more clearly.

The last of the Four Noble Truths refers to the 'Noble Eightfold Path', described as being an exemplary way to live life and fundamental in helping to remove Dukkha from our lives. It reinforces the parallels of a moral ethic with other faith communities and is described as ultimately leading to enlightenment – the self-realisation of the nature of all beings. The Eightfold Path is: Right Understanding (or view), Right Thought (or attitude), Right Speech, Right Action, Right Livelihood, Right Effort, Right Mindfulness and Right Concentration.

I have taken an intellectual and moral understanding of Buddhism into my life. I have found a method to help in understanding it, with its inevitable ups and downs. Buddhism is articulated for the benefit of anyone who has the ear to listen. The Western craving for success as a way to justify life is clearly misguided, and a lesson I have taken on board as the result of my change in direction. Is the change as fundamental as it appears on the surface? In Buddhism tolerance and compassion are implicit as they are in other faiths. Nothing like success succeeds in tying us to this world. Remove our obsessions with deep convictions, fundamental principles, immutable laws, inalienable rights and our insufferable egos and you remove the illusions of life.

Crossing Boundaries – A Hindu-Christian Biographical Reflection

Arani Sen

> The BJP in India. The BNP in England. The first would define me by my religious heritage, the latter by the colour of my skin. I believe in Hindu philosophy. I am not religious. I am a pacifist. I am a British Asian. My identity and my history are defined only by myself – beyond politics, beyond nationality, beyond religion and Beyond Skin. [1]

These words by the singer-songwriter, Niten Sawhney, resonated strongly with my own experiences of growing up in a context of constantly crossing boundaries. Like Sawhney, I was born and raised in England at a time when widespread multiculturalism was still a relatively new phenomenon. My parents came from India, from Calcutta to be precise. They are proud to be Bengali, with its intellectual, cultural, liberal heritage, which is the hub of their identity. They are Hindu, high caste (Ksatriya). Yet they have lived most of their life in England, in many ways living a Western middle-class lifestyle, in others retaining many cultural practices from India. This marks the start of my journey.

As Sawhney grapples, through his writing and music, with what it means to be Indian in Britain, he raises fundamental questions about identity which have pervaded my life. Where we differ is that, for Sawhney, identity is construed as 'beyond religion'; for myself, identity is very much defined *through* religion. This chapter forms a kind of theological reflection on my journey as a British Indian, of Hindu parentage, who is now an Anglican priest.

I grew up in an almost entirely white context, in the 1960s and 70s.

My father served as a GP in a mining village, and hence had considerable social status. This created something of a complexity at infant school as I was in a situation where I was the only Indian, and one of very few middle-class children. This made me a stranger at school, by virtue of my colour (in the days well before racist taunts were outlawed) and because of my social class. This was compounded by the fact that, in India, children would only mix with their own class or caste, society being highly delineated, and that affected whom I would socialise with. At the age of eight I was moved to a Nonconformist public school, thereby alienating me completely from my village context.

As a child, therefore, I grew up feeling different. For a start, I was a different colour from everyone else and this made me very noticeable. This is not an issue today, when I am proud to be British Asian but, as a child, it was a big issue. At times, though certainly not predominantly, it led me to feel that I was a stranger in my home country. It was the only country I knew, and I when I visited India, aged five, 10 and 15, it felt an alien country, socially, culturally and economically. Aged 10, in Calcutta, I was haunted by the images of displacement and poverty I could see from every window, of shanty towns and scantily-clad homeless children, while we stayed in relative comfort with servants tending to our every need. Such experiences were undoubtedly formative in my faith journey.

At primary school I made a very conscious decision, as did many of my fellow British Asians in their schools, that I would only speak English. Until then, I had been bilingual, Bengali-English, but now I decided I did not want to be different from my classmates. After all, they did not speak Bengali. In many different ways I had decided which cultural path I would follow, requesting English food for example. Of course I regret this now, but such is child psychology, especially in a context when all images in school, and all history taught are white. Indians had been a colonial people and now were the 'Third World'. How could I relate positively to that? Yet through all this, I moved daily between the Indian and English world. I could never avoid it. My parents remained Bengali, I was Bengali; nothing could change this.

The rest of the chapter will concentrate on my experiences of crossing religious boundaries, fundamental to my identity and to my relationship with Hinduism. As Moorhouse [2] elucidates, Bengali Hindus are proud of their liberal, thinking tradition, as well as their spiritual heritage. Above all, the values that have been instilled in me are of tolerance and a lack of dogmatism, very much Hindu hallmarks. As Lipner indicates, Hinduism allows one to find God in one or a variety of ways: 'Hinduism is a way of life, a collection of religions, a complex culture, one yet many'. [3] Although outwardly positive, it proved equally problematic as, although I was conscious of being Hindu, I did not find Hinduism easy to relate to. Even religious commentators do not shy away from the 'enormous complexity of this multi-faceted reality'. [4]

Hinduism to my parents is a way of life, and so it was for me growing up. Hinduism is in its essence monotheistic, yet worship is through thousands of gods, each family having its own particular gods to aid their worship. Hinduism is all-encompassing; Christianity, in its belief that salvation comes only through Jesus Christ, may seem arrogant to Hindus. [5] As Roger Hooker observes, a Hindu prayer room, traditionally part of every home, allows a picture of the Good Shepherd alongside Hindu gods and goddesses.

I grew up with a notion that God existed. I learned to pray to God but I did not use images. We had images of Ganesh and Shiva in the house, as well as pictures of the Pope and the Buddha. Each night my father brought out of the wardrobe an image of Kali, to aid him in his prayers. This image did affect me: it elicited fear, in that Kali holds in one of her four hands a severed head, dripping blood, which marks control of the unruly elements and violence in human lives [6]; but she also holds the sword of wisdom and makes reassuring gestures. Although the image itself did not aid me, I was helped to interpret a God of justice and a God of love through this. My mother would implore Durga,[7] the great goddess worshipped at the Pujas, to keep us safe as we travelled.

The Durga Puja is the great Bengali festival. As there were no Hindu temples in Britain at that time, the 1960s, I experienced the communal aspects of Hinduism only on my visits to India. Calcutta is awash with colour and new saris abound as the Puja celebrates Durga's return to her parental home, a time to relax and enjoy life when all Calcutta joins in this time of great joy, celebration and party. The goddess has triumphed over evil. [8] The nearest to this in Christianity is Christmas, when the Incarnation of Jesus is celebrated, as Jesus, the Son of God, enters our world to triumph over evil once and for all. In the West the religious significance has often been lost, but not in India. This is when Indian hospitality comes into its own: doors are open and huge meals are shared. This communal aspect, although part of the Christian tradition of the church as a community, the Body of Christ, [9] has been lost in the West and we can learn much from the East in this regard. There are many symbols, too: light over darkness, incense to draw us into God's presence, bells to call us to worship and icons are found within different Christian traditions such as Orthodoxy and Catholicism, and I have come to appreciate them as part of the Christian heritage.

Yet each day I would continue to cross religious boundaries. At school daily chapel was purely Christian, perhaps with some moral tales thrown in. We would sing hymns to praise God and hear Bible readings. The latter did not attract my attention, it was the Authorised Version and seemed distant from everyday life. Nevertheless, I possessed a very good knowledge of Bible stories, through RE lessons and Sunday school, (to which my parents had sent me, another sign of Hindu tolerance). I continued to believe in God, in a deity, but had no real understanding about who Jesus was. If anything, I felt Christian as much as I felt Hindu, although I was excluded from the Sacrament of Holy Communion.

Where I struggled with Hinduism was in the area of caste and rebirth, particularly the belief that there could be an 'outcaste', the Dalits, ritually *untouchables*. An excerpt from a recent Indian novel expresses the ritual nature and harsh realities of being 'untouchable':

> Pappachi would not allow Paravars[10] into the house. Nobody would. They were not allowed to touch anything that touchables touched … Mammachi told Estha and Rahel that she could remember a time in her girlhood when Paravans were not allowed to walk on public roads, not

allowed to cover their upper bodies, not allowed to carry umbrellas. They had to put their hands over their mouths when they spoke, to divert their polluted breath away from those whom they addressed. [11]

I myself have studied Dalit experiences in India, visiting villagers and hearing at first hand people's experiences, and the above is far from fiction. As an adult I have reconnected with India, a place where I recognise my roots. Yet, although my parents and other enlightened Hindus are embarrassed by caste, it is undeniably pivotal to Hindu culture and has even permeated the church, although the church is now at the forefront of instigating change. [12]

By the time I was a teenager, I found that I could not incorporate a system whereby, in the words of the prophet Amos, the needy are trampled on and 'ruin is brought to the poor of the land'. [13] Somehow I fathom that, at the heart of Hinduism, there exists a sense that your life situation is your *karma*, a kind of fatalism, and that things cannot improve. Despite all government initiatives there seems to be an inherent reluctance to alleviate poverty and caste from India: 'the elites in India defend their position on religious grounds, claiming that a person's position on the social hierarchy is a direct reward for his merits in his past life'. [14]

A Christian hope, a hope of sight for the blind and freedom for the captive, identifies my faith to this day and is cardinal to my own ministry. It is marked by an understanding that God is a God of love, who interacts with humanity to the extent that he himself has suffered and died on the cross and therefore is fully involved in human suffering. As Moltmann powerfully depicts in *The Crucified God:* [15]

> Anyone who cries out to God in his suffering echoes the death cry of the dying Christ, the Son of God ... in a profound way senses the human God, who cries out for me and intercedes for him with his cross, where man in his torment is dumb.

Yet the Christian story does not end with God crucified but continues because Christ was raised, and therefore death was overcome. This is, in Moltmann's theology of hope, 'the definitive event of eschatological promise', [16] a promise that offers wounded humanity hope for a better world.

The theology of the Kingdom of God, which Jesus inaugurated and commanded us to continue, begins with the story of God interacting with humanity, through Jesus' incarnation into the world, in human time and history. It is the story of Jesus, fully human and fully God, who moved on earth, suffered as we do, experienced human emotions, yet who was able to perform miraculous signs of the kingdom, healing the sick, giving dignity to the poor, and ultimately defeating death through resurrection. His command to the disciples to 'proclaim the kingdom of God and to heal' is equally applicable to Christians today who are called to work together in bringing about God's Kingdom *now* (not just looking forward to the *not yet* and therefore not getting involved in the world). For this purpose Jesus has given his Holy Spirit as a sign that his ministry is active in the world today: 'But you will receive power when the Holy Spirit has come upon you, and you will be my witnesses in Jerusalem, in all Judea and Samaria and to the ends of the earth'. [17]

In terms of the search for salvation, I find divergences between Christianity and Hinduism. Hinduism proposes a spiritual search for 'oneness with God', encompassing in its complexity both birth and rebirth. Borrowing from the Hindu concept of *dharma*, Hooker propounds that Christians, in this scheme, are on a 'lower spiritual level'. [18] Fundamentally, he argues that Christians are unable to keep stillness, but preoccupy themselves with business. Above all, they seem to separate the figure of Christ from the self. Christianity does not propose a *search for* peace with God, although the meditative tradition is essential, [19] but rather the peace is offered to us, through the death and resurrection of Jesus Christ:

> Therefore since we are justified by faith, we have peace with God through our Lord Jesus Christ, through whom we have attained access to this grace in which we stand; and we boast in our hope of sharing in the glory of God. [20]

My own encounter with Jesus Christ was unashamedly evangelical yet does not negate any of my faith journey, very briefly set out in this chapter. Simply, one night when I was an undergraduate, Jesus Christ met with me, in a mysterious yet powerful way. My faith journey was no longer a search for God, but God had encountered me in the revelation of his Son. The theologian, Karl Barth, expresses the active, hypostatic relationship thus:

> In a bridging of the gulf (from God's side) between divine and human comprehensibility it comes to pass that within the sphere and within the limits of comprehensibility, there is a true knowledge of God's essence generally and hence also of the Triunity. [21]

As I connect with my Bengali roots, I reflect on my long and complex relationship with Hinduism. Naturally, the missionary spirit of Christianity proves incompatible with Hindu tolerance and openness. Pannekar poses the fundamental question:

> The Christian desires that the Hindu become a Christian. Hinduism has no such wish to make Christians Hindu – to the Hindu, in fact, one cannot become what one is not; yet Hinduism will prevent Hindus from being unfaithful to their *dharma*. Is there any solution to the problem? [22]

This is a question to which there is no easy answer and one with which I have been grappling for many years. As I continue to minister in strongly multi-faith contexts it is something I will have to continue to grapple with, as we seek to accept one another in our beliefs. Pannekar reminds us that such a process transcends trite discussion or pure rational knowledge and demands a fundamental respect for one another, for a search for the source of each other's faiths. In the end, we are not called to compromise what we believe, but to begin with the premise of the mystery of God:

> I have been found by those who did not seek me
> I have shown myself to those who did not ask for me. [23]

References

1. Niten Sawhney, sleeve notes to the Album *Beyond Skin*, London: Outcaste Records Ltd, London 1999.
2. G Moorhouse, *Calcutta*, London: Orion, 1998, ch 6.
3. J Lipner, *Hindus: Their religious views and practices,* London: Routledge, 1994, p 5.
4. Lipner p 2.

5. R Hooker, 'Learning from other faiths' in C Lamb and R Hooker *Love the Stranger*, London: SPCK, 1986.

6. Lipner, p 286.

7. Durga and Kali are synonymous.

8. Lipner p 300.

9. I Corinthians 12:27.

10. Paravars are a Dalit *jati:* within each of the four *Varnas*: Brahmin, Ksatriya, Vaisyas, Sudras, there exist hundreds of sub-castes or *jatis*.

11. Arundhati Roy, *The God of Small Things,* London: Fortress, 1997.

12. Dalit theology is the major Christian theology coming out of India since the 1980s.

13. Amos 8:4.

14. V Samuel, quoted in C Sugden, *Seeking the Asian face of Jesu*s, Oxford: Regnum, 1997.

15. J Moltmann, *The Crucified God*, London: SCM, 1974, p 252.

16. J Moltmann, *Theology of Hope* SPCK London, 1967 p19.

17. Acts 1: 8.

18. R Hooker, 'Learning from other faiths' in C Lamb and R Hooker *Love the Stranger*, London: SPCK, 1986.

19. Here a great deal can be learned from Hinduism, eg De Mello.

20. Romans 5:1-2.

21. K Barth, *Church Dogmatics* 1:1, London: T & T Clark, 1975, p 371.

22. R Pannekar, 'The Unknown Christ of Hinduism' in J Hick and B Hebblethwaite, *Chrisitianity and other Religions,* Glasgow: Collins, 1980, p124.

23. Romans 10:20.

Bridging a Divide – 'Passing over the Ganges'

David A Hart

It was in 1978 at Oxford University that I heard John Dunne rehearse in his Sarum lectures his arguments advocating the practice of 'passing over' from one's own religious tradition into another, as a means of furthering both one's own understanding of and one's commitment to the other's religious faith. Thereby, he argued, one would both deepen and broaden one's spiritual sensibilities.

It took me another 20 years before I had the opportunity myself to put this theory into practice in my life, in relation to specifically the Hindu tradition. Of course, Bede Griffiths had been a pioneer of this for the generation before, in setting up Christian/Hindu ashrams in Ashekadin. My generation have the unique opportunity to perform a 'marriage of east and west' without leaving these shores.

For myself, I did manage to combine short visits to India with more regular visits to my local Hindu temple in the East Midlands, specific study of the Sanskrit language, the Bhagavad Gita and the Vedas, combined with growing personal friendships with Hindus of my acquaintance who when they knew I was interested would invite me to their festivals.

Perhaps I should not have been so surprised by the warmth of my welcome there. After all, the British and Indians have had a fairly dynamic symbiotic relationship with each other for over two centuries, and share many similar cultural views and priorities. To some extent, 'Hinduism' is a British categorisation of what European colonisers discovered in Indian religious practice, while Christianity within India is virtually an indigenous religion dating back to the arrival of St Thomas in Cranganore in 54 AD. As Arundhati Roy has put it: 'Christianity seeps into India like tea from a tea-bag'. So the English Channel and the Indian Ocean have ebbed and flowed into each other and still do in 2002!

What I have discovered in my own post-colonial pilgrimages to India is an overwhelming personal realisation of overlap between Christianity as I have learned it from my mother's knee and Hinduism as I am discovering it from my studies and Hindu friends in adult life.

The scriptures are manifold and written over millennia. There is no single view of God, Elohim abound as *devi*. The mythologies are complex and interwoven, but in the Ramayana and Mahabharata we appear to have an equivalent Indian foundation-story to the wanderings of the people of Israel as depicted in the Bible. Whether the wanderers are divine or human seems irrelevant to the main issue of how they accept and alter the destinies that come their way through parentage and chance.

Krishna as Christ personifies many of the struggles of a personal identity that Everyman knows, and his story becomes paradigmatic for the believer. The festivals mark the seasons of the year and also divide human lives conveniently as, I hope, do the chapters in this book. Diwali-like Christmas focuses on the lighting of lamps at a time of the year that seems dark, and provides an opportunity for families to buy one another sweets and clothes and clean their homes so hospitality can be offered to family and friends. In each case, the proof of the plum pudding is in the sparkle in the children's eyes! And these festivals do not require participants to accept much dogma to enjoy them I realised this in 1992 on the Feast of Makara Sankranti (the Repentant Crocodile) flying home-made kites on a Gujarati rooftop.

As I glanced to either side of me while attempting to fly my kite higher, I saw that my neighbours were Muslim and Hindu. No one religion's kites were flying any higher than their neighbours': hence the limitation of the descriptor I had read - 'Hindu festival'.

As far as liturgical prayers go, there is, of course, the problem of choice of language. For all my current efforts, I will never have the sort of familiarity with the daily-recited Gayatri Mantra in Sanskrit that I have with the Lord's Prayer in its Elizabethan English. On the other hand, familiarity can breed contempt, so I have no hesitation, whenever I glimpse it, of praising the sun as my brother, as did St Francis, or, as the mantra has it:

> *Om. Bhura bhuva swah, tatsavitur varenyam bhargo devasya dhimahi dhaiyo yo nah vrachodayat.*

O God, the Giver of life, Remover of pain and sorrows, Bestower of Happiness, and Creator of the Universe, Thou are most luminous, pure and adorable. We meditate on Thee. May Thou inspire and illuminate our minds.

Within temple and church, the pundit/priest leads recitations on behalf of the gathered congregation. *Arti* and the Eucharist for me are virtually indistinguishable as focuses of prayer to God, led by the priest who blesses God and the people. In certain circumstances a layperson can lead the ceremony also. Bread and wine, *pradesh*, are received as sacramental tokens of our common human/divine sustenance: anyone present at the ceremony is invited to receive of God's food if they so wish.

Ethics is the attempt to relate our religious beliefs to our social practice and so is a vital litmus test for any religion. It is no accident that the greatest admiration that Mahatma Gandhi had for Christianity was focused on Jesus' teachings in the Sermon on the Mount. For a contemporary ethics developing insights from that sermon, I turn now as much to the *Bhagavad Gita* as to Don Cupitt's *Solar Ethics*. They each provide guidelines to the reader in making vital choices in a world of conflicting interests where I simply have to choose between one good and another: to take arms and fight and thereby to injure and kill, or to rest and thereby evade my responsibilities as a citizen. My responsibilities are mine alone to choose 'in fear and trembling', as Kierkegaard and Gandhi each realised in the lonely decisions they had to take.

At the heart of Christianity and Hinduism I find a god within emphasised, not only in the scriptures but also in the ethos of the faith as it is lived and taught today. Christianity teaches that God forsook his position of power to become incarnate in a humble Palestinian child – thus the value of each human being made in God's very image, male and female. Hindus in their symbolic greeting of the other person 'namskara', with hands brought together in respectful salutation, recognise the divinity in every stranger they meet and thereby also follow the Athanasian Creed line: 'God became human in order that humans could become divine'.

In a radical understanding of each of these faiths, the boundaries of status and caste dissolve in front of the truth of the divine-human admixture in each unique human person, regardless of race or beliefs.

As I am currently a priest without a specific parochial responsibility, at 11 o'clock on a Sunday morning in Derby, you can find me either in the cathedral or in the Hindu temple in Normanton. There is no overriding factor which will take me to one rather than another … except perhaps the calendar. On Diwali I am likely to be in Normanton, but for Christmas I shall be in the cathedral. Perhaps that is because when those buildings are full, and the message comes over strongest, we can rejoice at the fellowship that gathers around the proclaimed story of our faith. For myself, I now know that each of these faiths has become part of my own understanding of who I am, and I am grateful for the opportunity both fellowships of believers have offered me, to join their family and become one of them.

What We Might Think and How We Might Act – Diplomacy, Challenge and Exploration in Multi-Faith Britain

Paul Weller

The essays in this book reflect on what, as people of diverse backgrounds, we might think and also how we might act, in contemporary multi-faith Britain. The essays in the first part of the book primarily reflect on how historically inherited religious traditions and beliefs have themselves developed through the engagement with the challenges posed by religious plurality. The essays in the second part of the book are written in a more personal register, exploring the implications of this evolving religious plurality for the beliefs, commitments, lives and work of individuals. The purpose of this concluding paper is to try to provide an overview that both picks up on a number of themes from the contributions made by authors in earlier papers, while also seeking to contextualise these themes and to make a contribution of its own.

The context of multi-faith Britain

Religion has today re-emerged onto the public stage of Britain. This has happened in a way that perhaps would have seemed unlikely during the revolutionary days of the 1960s, when it was commonly thought that religion would soon no longer be significant for public life and might even fade away completely. But this re-emergence of religion has also been connected with the development of religious plurality in ways that were not generally foreseen. One key example that illustrates how far the context of this new century differs from the general expectations of the 1960s is the inclusion of a question on religious affiliation in the 2001 census.

The inclusion of a religion question in the decennial census indicates the degree to which religion now forms an important part of the social policy agenda of a culturally and religiously plural society. New questions are only added to the census after a great deal of debate and the articulation of an adequate 'business case' in relation to expressed needs for such information on the part of local and national Government, business and academia. A religion question had previously been included in censuses of Northern Ireland, where issues of religion and equal opportunities have long been part of the political agenda, but this has not been the case in England, Scotland and Wales. Therefore the inclusion of such a question across the United Kingdom as a whole signals the way in which the role of religion has come to be re-evaluated in relation to issues of public life, and especially in relation to the appropriateness of the public services provided to diverse population groups along with the role of religious communities, groups and organisations in the provision of such services.

The ways in which the religion question was asked was also significant. The detailed form of the question in Northern Ireland differed from that asked for the first time in Scotland, and the form of the question in Scotland also differed from that in England and Wales. But what all the variations of the question had in common was that they did not ask about religious belief as such, but about the identification of individuals with a particular religion. The options that were offered/prompted for response, as well as those that were not flagged up as such, should be noted. When the census results derived from the religion question are published, it is will be important to try to evaluate the effect of the form of the question upon the results of the exercise. In the version of the question asked in England and Wales, respondents were asked to choose from the options of 'None', Christian, Buddhist, Hindu, Jewish, Muslim or Sikh, or else to write in the name of any 'other' religion.

The pilot exercise undertaken by the Office for National Statistics yielded some perhaps surprising indications of what might emerge from the census itself. First of all respondents were, on the whole, more willing to answer the question on religion than another new question that related to levels of personal income. In addition, respondents were more likely to opt to identify themselves with a religion than might have been expected in a society where an ethos of secularity (as distinct from an ideology of secularism) has become quite widespread and permeative.

To this extent, the results of the religion question may well underline the new public significance of religion in multi-faith Britain. At the same time, the particular categories offered to respondents underlines the potential of this exercise for oversimplifying and reifying what might, in reality, be a much more complex and fluid set of lived religious identities. For example, during the Office for National Statistics' consultation process that preceded the decision to include a religion question in the census, it was pointed out that the options as offered are unlikely to match the lived religious realities of at least that section of the population of over 100,000 people of Chinese ethnic origin. Among people of Chinese origins who are not Christians, elements of Buddhism, Taoism, and Confucianism all combine with indigenous traditions of veneration of the ancestors in ways that make an answer to the religious question in the census something that is far from straightforward.

The difficulty presented by the census question for people of Chinese origins may also be the case for the perhaps still relatively small but also growing numbers of people in 'mixed-faith' families, as well as for individuals whose religious identity is consciously formed by an attempt to live in the light of more than one religious tradition. In addition, the framing of the question in terms of any particular 'religion' (even if the write-in 'other' is chosen) or 'none' will have presented difficulties of response for those sections of the population for whom spirituality is a key aspect of their personal identities, but who do not identify with any particular institutional or historical forms of religion.

Developments such as the inclusion of a religion question in the census underline the significance of religion, and the recognition of its plurality, in contemporary public life. But the context for this is clearly also connected with a recognition on the part of government, the wider society, and to some degree among the religions themselves, of the historically ambiguous potential of the roles that can be played by religions in the public sphere. It is the historical ambiguity of religions which means that their re-emergence into the public life of Britain is distinguished by a concern for what might be characterised as 'religious diplomacy'.

Dialogue as diplomacy

In the context of the impact of globalisation and the decline of the nation state and of social class as key markers of personal and corporate identity, religions can act as important alternative forms of identification. As such they can provide individuals and groups with a sense of 'belonging' that is capable of making connections between the local and the global within what can otherwise be experienced as the potentially quite destabilising social, personal and epistemological fluidity of (post)modern life.

In highly diverse societies, it is generally perceived to be necessary to find a number of commonly agreed principles and some agreed practices that can be used to provide the working foundations for integrating the diversities within a social organism that can function at least reasonably well. Because of the historical continuities and relative stability that the religions embody, they are seen as significant players in civil society with the potential to make creative contributions to the identification and promotion of the key common values and procedures necessary for undergirding a shared social sense of mutual belonging. The governmental powers-that-be recognise this potential contribution of religions and seek to draw upon it to help meet the challenge of integration in a highly diverse society, while religions themselves see in this recognition an opportunity for exerting some influence in public life.

On the other hand, alongside the recognition of the positive contribution that religions can make to values agendas, there is widespread concern that religions and their diverse and competing claims can also have a serious potential for either igniting new social conflicts or inflaming old ones. Because of the kind of claims that, historically, religions have made, once they either initiate or legitimate social conflicts the form that these conflicts take can be informed by a particular vehemence and intensity. In addition, because of the absolutising tendency within many religions, at least a degree of intractability can be encountered in attempts to resolve such conflicts.

The transmutation of religious identities into the service of an 'identity politics' can lead to the absolutisation of such identities in ways that can all too easily result in projects for the 'religious cleansing' of those with 'other' identities. Such projects can take shape in forms of proselytism that, while eschewing violence and legal suppression, nevertheless in psychological, social and religious terms deny the 'other' their religious freedom to be themselves. Alternatively, in more extreme cases, such projects can take the forms of a physical violence that attempted during the Nazi occupation of Europe and the more recent events in Bosnia-Herzogovina to carry out a 'religious cleansing' through the enforced geographical displacement of the religious 'other' and/or their liquidation.

It is for all these reasons that, on the part of Government and among religious communities and organisations themselves, that at least some degree of shared interest has emerged in what might be characterised as 'dialogue as diplomacy'. Dialogue as diplomacy has its limitations, of course. It can become a club in which only the 'liberal' in each tradition are invited to participate, and which can thereby become disconnected from the possibility of exerting influence upon the heartlands of the religions, or the power centres of the wider world's realpolitik. At its worst, dialogue as diplomacy can potentially become not only irrelevant but also dangerous, both for religions themselves and for the wider society. This can occur when dynamic and diverse religious traditions are unjustifiably reified into what are actually phantasms of unified communities that are made to bear more weight and significance than the degree of commonalities of interest and perspective that do exist can support. Such reification can, in turn, develop into types of communalism in which forms of religious practice ranging from the self-indulgent to the unjust are allowed to continue unchallenged on the grounds of a superficially conducted politics of respectful co-existence.

Whatever its limitations, however, dialogue as diplomacy is not to be sneered at or undervalued. It is surely better to talk with other people than to kill them. It is better to be polite to them than to ignore them. It is better to offer an invitation and hospitality than to freeze out or ignore the 'other'. However, even at its best, dialogue as diplomacy may not be sufficient in engaging with the challenges facing both the religions and the society of multi-faith Britain.

Dialogue as challenge

While there may well be a necessary diplomacy in relation to the nature and place of religious plurality in public life, a more rounded engagement with the implications of religious plurality entails elements of 'challenge' as well as of affirmation. Such elements of challenge are of importance and significance both for the religions themselves and for the wider society in which they are set.

Religions, albeit in a variety of forms, all bear witness to the importance of things that cannot be seen, touched, smelled, tasted and heard, but which they nevertheless claim are essential for a more balanced perspective on what is experienced in these ways. Therefore when the governmental powers-that-be invite religions to contribute to building a values consensus for the promotion of social cohesion, it may well be that, in the end, they will not be so comfortable with the values that the religions actually do bring to bear.

Religions have important – albeit often significantly differing – things to contribute about, for example, values in relation to families and their role within society. Contributions of this kind are likely to be welcomed by the powers-that-be in the context of general concerns about the creation of stable environments within which children and young people might be able to grow into mature participation in the rights and responsibilities of society. But it is less clear how welcome might be the perspectives of those religious values that, in service of visions of justice and, perhaps especially, of economic justice, disturb and challenge the status quo.

In relation to Britain as a whole, the contemporary political and economic landscape is one in which, while there are political and economic differences among the mainstream political parties, no real alternatives are being offered by them to the dominant and underlying global economic system of market capitalism. Religions, however, remain a reminder that the way in which our society lives and organises itself is neither natural nor inevitable, nor is it the only possible way for a society to be but, rather, it is the way that a society has chosen for itself. In this context, religions, in so far as they allow themselves to be informed and shaped by the originating visions embodied within them, can offer important alternative visions to profit, unlimited consumption and notions of endless progress as the criteria by which social life is constituted.

At the same time, the plurality of contemporary British society also brings disturbance to the religions themselves. In comparison with those times and places in which religions were more or less identified with specific social and/or geographical spaces, it is now far less possible for religions to continue to operate undisturbed within their own immediate spheres of thinking and doing.

Of course, the religions have always had to face the challenges that arise from the diversities that exist within each religion. However, even though the upheavals resulting from such challenges have often been quite profound, they have nevertheless been limited by the fact that even the most radical of such challenges and transformations have occurred within an horizon in which at least some basic metaphysical and epistemological perspectives were shared by the major protagonists. The challenges arising from the internal diversities that have been defined as 'deviant' or 'heretical' may, historically, have been seen by the religions as potentially more disturbing than the challenges of diversity that come from those who are perceived as the completely religious 'other'. But in relation even to sharp internal conflicts, the shared presuppositions that have remained a part of the common 'language' and 'grammar' of a particular religion underline how different are the challenges facing religions that arise from an engagement with the diverse beliefs and practices of the religiously external 'other'.

In the encounter with the other, a number of commonalities are often perceived, at least at the level of the lived religious experience of individuals, families and groups. Such commonalities also pose a question about what distinctiveness there might be within particular religions. In the light of this, it becomes necessary for each religion to try to find a way within the logic, the 'language' and the 'grammar' of its own tradition, to try to find satisfactory and appropriate ways to account both for the commonality and for the distinctiveness. This process often entails at least some degree of the reinvention of tradition, the radicality or otherwise of which can have an impact on the extent to which reinvention is received and internalised, or otherwise, by the broad constituency of the wider religious tradition.

Some religions, of course, already have an approach to religious plurality in which the plurality has itself already been a part of the self-understanding of the particular religion. But, whatever their starting point in relation to the challenges arising from the increasingly experienced fact of religious plurality, all religions in common continue to face the challenges that arise from secularity. Despite the re-emergence of religions in the public sphere, the challenge of the secular has far from gone away, although perhaps it now takes a different form from that in which it was found for much of the last century.

While atheism and secularism as systematised epistemologies and integrated ways of life were once sponsored by the states and political systems that were spawned by Marxist-Leninist ideology, they are now particularly the preserve of committed groups of individuals. At the same time, the ethos of secularity as a background to modern life has arguably become even more permeative than it once was. The challenges arising to religions from such secularity are not so much those of the forms of explicit ideological conflict that religious believers once faced in the Communist-ruled countries of Central and

Eastern Europe. They are now perhaps more to do with perceptions of the irrelevance of organised religions to the life concerns and perspectives of large numbers of people. Such secularity is very much part of the plurality of contemporary Britain, which is perhaps more accurately characterised as both a multi-faith and a secular society.

The secular element of contemporary plurality continues to challenge and interrogate all religions. There is no refuge for religions in the formation of illusory 'religious unity fronts' over and against the ethos of secularity. Those forms of religions that attempt to avoid engagement with the challenges posed by secularity are likely to find that they are increasingly marginalised from the wider society in which all the religions are located.

The challenge of secularity means, at the very least, that religions have to begin to learn to live in the field of tension between commitment and uncertainty. Without an embracing of the element of plurality as challenge in the various dimensions outlined above, then for both the wider society and for religions themselves, dialogue as diplomacy can all too easily become the domestication and instrumentalisation of dialogue. Dealing with the implications of contemporary religious plurality, however, calls not only for an engagement with dialogue as diplomacy and dialogue as challenge, but is likely also to find itself engaged in dialogue as exploration. The dynamic of dialogue itself leads this way.

Dialogue as exploration

The establishment of trust to enable exchange needs the etiquette of religious relations expressed in dialogue as diplomacy. The truthfulness necessary to inform a dialogue that is not domesticated leads to the willingness to engage in dialogue as challenge. But perhaps it is only possible to evolve a workable creative tension between dialogue as diplomacy and dialogue as challenge if the dynamic of dialogue as exploration is also embraced. Such dialogical exploration can take place in a number of ways and has a variety of dimensions.

First of all, opportunities for the study of religion within the public education system can provide a sphere in which it is possible to have a free space for exploration without the prerequisite of commitment. Secondly, there is the importance to dialogue of that which is signified by the word 'spirituality', and which is concerned with an aspect of experience found both within and beyond the boundaries of structured religious traditions, communities and organisations.

The educational project within public institutions is one that is, of necessity, different from education undertaken within religious traditions and communities. The diversity of religions in contemporary society is increasingly reflected in the syllabuses of both schools and higher education institutions. In the public sphere, education for the development of religious literacy can no longer justifiably be conducted on the basis of a 'we' that is assumed in some sense to share a single and dominant religio-cultural tradition.

In a society that is characterised both by secularity and the diversity of religions, for the study of religion to be engaged and effective it needs to operate on the basis of an inclusive 'we' that embraces pupils and students from a wide variety of religious and secular backgrounds. At the same time, and without returning to confessionalist pedagogical assumptions, the development of a proper religious literacy entails the identification of ways of facilitating pupils and students in understanding the significance of religions by learning from the challenges posed by religions, as well as by learning things about them.

The public education system as an arena to guarantee and enable free and critical exploration of the significance of religions remains something that is of great importance for the future of religions in a plural society. Its role is distinct from, and complementary to, what also remains the necessary pedagogical responsibility for formation within the religious traditions that belongs to the task of the religious communities, groups and organisations.

One of the lesser-known aspects of the Education Act currently governing the whole school curriculum in England and Wales is that part of its preamble refers to an overall aim of education being concerned with 'spiritual development'. Religious Education and the study of religions focus primarily on the historical phenomena of religions. But the recognition in a primarily secular document of a dimension of human experience that is concerned with 'spiritual development' is something that is of significance for the religiously plural environment of contemporary Britain. Religion has re-emerged into the public sphere. At significant points religion can overlap with spirituality, but a concern with spirituality is found in places far beyond the boundaries of organised religion. Sometimes what is experienced as 'religion' and what is signified by the word 'spirituality' can be separated by a yawning chasm. This can occur when religion becomes reduced either to stultifying habit and conventionality, or else becomes an identity politics that is concerned primarily with its own rights rather than with the spiritual roots by which the historical manifestations of all religions are ultimately to be judged.

It is, in the end, those dimensions of religion signalled by the phenomenon of 'spirituality' that speak to the religions from beyond their historical forms and are the ultimate rationale for their existence. These dimensions also sustain the important capacity of religions for self-criticism and radical renewal – a capacity that has been evidenced over the centuries as prophetic figures have arisen who have judged their own religions from within in as strong, if not stronger terms, as those mounting critiques from outside.

The frequent imprecision with which the word 'spirituality' is used can be connected with an at least questionable moral and intellectual laziness. But at the same time it is invoked because those who use the word, whether within or outside of religious traditions and communities, wish to indicate that there exists a dimension of life that is not susceptible to reductionism. The sub-title of this book is 'an experiment in worship'. This seemed, at least initially, a somewhat puzzling, and perhaps potentially misleading sub-title for this book. As will by now be clear from the contributions of the authors before this one, the essays only occasionally and tangentially touch upon religious worship either in individual religions, or else in terms of what is often popularly labelled 'multi-faith worship' or more carefully described as 'shared observance'.

But on further reflection, it is perhaps entirely appropriate for a book concerned with religious plurality in contemporary Britain to be sub-titled in this way. This is because the category, and even more so the practice, of 'worship' is something that is concerned with opening up the spaces in individual and corporate experience that the word 'spirituality' is intended to signify and keep them open for exploration.

One example of the interface between the re-emergence of religion into public life in the context of religious plurality and the dimension of 'worship' was a 'Shared Act of Reflection and Commitment' that took place in the Palace of Westminster to mark the new Millennium. This drew together contributions from representatives of a range of the religious traditions that make up contemporary British society. The event grew out of a consultative process in which both the Government office charged with co-ordinating Millennium events, the Archbishop of Canterbury's office at Lambeth Palace, the Interfaith Network, and representatives of various religious groups had all been involved. It also emerged against the background of the debates that had taken place over what elements should be included, and in what way, in what eventually became the 'Faith Zone' of the Greenwich Millennium Dome.

In the past, religious events marking the key occasions in state and society in Britain have taken place in the context of acts of worship led by representatives of, and conducted according to, the worship formularies and practices of the established Church of England. This was previously the case even where, as in more recent years, invitations have also been extended to representatives of other religions to be present as observers and/or as active participants through the contribution of readings, blessings or personal statements. For the first time, the Millennium 'shared observance' reflected at national level an organic process of development that has, at more local levels, been gathering momentum over the last decade of the last century. In these developments, the local state, local interfaith initiatives and organisations, and the dioceses of the Church of England have often combined to facilitate more religiously inclusive forms of observance and celebration, as for example to mark the appointment of mayors coming from other than Christian religious backgrounds.

Dialogue between religions – including also acts of worship or of 'shared observance' as outlined above, manifestly has 'uses', both for religions and for the wider society. Many of these are positive, and potentially also creative – certainly by contrast with their alternatives. But a purely instrumentalist approach to dialogue as diplomacy and dialogue as challenge can only, at most, be a truncated dialogue. Without an open engagement with the unconditioned with which religions claim to be ultimately concerned, such instrumentalist dialogue can also contain the seeds of a significant danger to the integrity of the religions. Some obligation to enter into dialogue as diplomacy and challenge is recognised by religions because of the impetus to give some historical expression to the ultimate and the unconditioned that are at the wellsprings of their tradition. But if the ultimate is rather made subservient to the penultimate, and the unconditioned to the conditioned, then religions can lose their integrity.

Spirituality and worship are concerned more with exploration than with definition. What we might think and how we might act in multi-faith Britain will, if we are prepared fully to engage with the implications of contemporary religious plurality and secularity, be characterised by a willingness to engage in dialogue in its distinct but complementary dimensions of diplomacy, challenge and exploration.